ACRL Publications in Librarianship no. 36

The Shaping of American Library Education

by

CHARLES D. CHURCHWELL

American Library Association

Chicago 1975

Library of Congress Cataloging in Publication Data

Churchwell, Charles D   1926–
    The shaping of American library education.

    (ACRL publications in librarianship; no. 36)
    Bibliography: p.
    Includes index.
    1. Library education—United States—History.
I. Title. II. Series: Association of College and
Research Libraries. ACRL publications in librarian-
ship; no. 36.
Z674.A75 no. 36 [Z668]   020'.8s [020'.711'73]   74–23989
ISBN 0-8389-0170-0

To my wife,
Yvonne, and daughters,
Linda and Cynthia

Contents

Acknowledgments

I am indebted to many people for assisting me with this book. I am grateful to Dean Robert B. Downs, Dr. Harold Goldstein, Mrs. Joann Kelly, Mrs. Kathleen Draper, and Mr. Ernest J. Reese for assisting me with much of the research and ideas in the book, which appeared first as a doctoral dissertation. I owe a very special thanks to Dr. Edward G. Holley for his initial and constant encouragement during the long period the manuscript was being prepared for publication, for without his help it is doubtful that I would have offered the manuscript to the Editorial Board for consideration. I am also grateful to Mrs. Esther Schrader for typing the manuscript, and to Mr. Herbert Bloom, Senior Editor, and Mrs. Bonnie Oberman, Editorial Assistant, for their helpful suggestions and professional assistance. And finally, I wish to thank all those who assisted me in important but intangible ways. The list of names is too long to cite, but Mr. Vernon S. Simpson, Ms. Geraldine Rickman, Dr. Donald Hendricks, Mr. Robert Oram, and Mr. Walter Smith played too significant a role not to be mentioned.

1. Introduction

Professional education for an occupation has always been a subsequent development of the occupation itself. As the knowledge of an occupation accumulated and its techniques became more complex, the methods of education evolved from that of apprenticeship programs, the earliest and simplest form of professional education, to the highly organized professional school. Professional education has become, therefore, the most widely used method of transmitting knowledge and techniques of an occupation from the skilled practitioner and theoretician to the unskilled beginner.

A brief examination of one of the world's oldest professions may illustrate this point. The first medical education in America, as elsewhere, was obtained by the student from the practicing doctor who taught him the knowledge and skills of medicine, and who allowed the student to pay for his education by washing bottles, mixing drugs, and assisting in such matters as bloodletting.[1] The student, by being present in the doctor's office and accompanying him on calls, learned the lore of diagnosis and therapy.[2] As time went on, an increase in the number of students seeking training, a growing medical practice, and an increase in medical knowledge and techniques compelled many doctors to abandon the apprenticeship method of education and to band

1

together and establish private medical schools.[3] At the same time, some colleges were establishing chairs of medicine and medical schools. Before the end of the eighteenth century, medical schools were established at the College of Philadelphia, King's College, Harvard College, and Dartmouth College.[4] During the nineteenth century, because the demand for doctors and the anticipation of personal profits were so great, the number of medical schools reached 162. But despite this rapid increase in the proprietary and university medical schools, the apprenticeship method did not disappear at once; rather the three types of medical education existed together and competed for a time.[5] However, with the opening of Johns Hopkins Medical School in 1893, and with the publication of the Carnegie report on medical education in 1910,[6] medical education—under the control of a university with the necessary hospital facilities and a medical faculty free to concentrate on teaching and research—became the ideal.[7] The era of apprenticeship and proprietary medical schools was gradually but definitely coming to an end.

Education for the other two oldest professions, theology and law, evolved in a manner similar to that of professional medical education. The students apprenticed themselves to a practicing lawyer or preacher and mastered the theory of law and theology by reading the legal and religious books in their preceptor's library and being questioned by the latter. Practical experience was gained by serving as legal clerks and ministerial aids. From these apprenticeship programs and activities, today's professional schools of law and theology had their beginnings.[8]

Education for librarianship, like that for medicine, law, and theology, has evolved through definite stages. This development, up to 1939, may be divided into three general periods. The first period covers library education before 1887, when all librarians in America were educated through the apprenticeship system. The would-be librarian joined the staff of a library and mastered the knowledge and techniques of librarianship by reading, observation, instruction, and performance of library work.

The second period spans the time from 1887, when the first library school was established at Columbia College, to the end of World War I. During this period the number of library schools increased from one to nineteen, taking their place alongside apprenticeship systems as centers of library education. These thirty-one years constituted the era when "education for librarianship kept equal pace with the foundation and growth of the

American library movement and contributed to current American library service much of its distinctive character."[9]

The twenty years between the two world wars encompass the third period of education for librarianship. During these two decades, 1919–39, several forces coalesced and compelled the American Library Association to exert a positive influence on the evolution of library education, raising it from the level of apprenticeship to a graduate and professional level under the aegis of colleges and universities. During this time, the Carnegie Corporation contributed great leadership and gave substantial financial assistance, attempting to do for library education what it had done for medical education twenty-five years earlier.

The first two stages of development have been treated in studies by four students of library education. The first of these, *Professional Education for Librarianship*, a Ph.D. dissertation by Tse-Chien Tai, was published in 1925. Tai's purpose for undertaking the study was to formulate a program for library education and present it as a detailed proposal for the establishment of a library school at Iowa State University.[10]

In order to create a framework for his proposal, Tai assumed that there was no systematic body of knowledge about the qualifications of librarians; therefore, the confusion and contradictions which had hampered discussions on library education before 1925 had been inevitable. He further assumed that a theoretical basis for such a body of knowledge could be formulated by analyses of the social, educational, and intellectual forces which produced libraries and determined the character of their service. These assumptions were substantiated by his historical study of "the training and education for librarianship and the origin and development of professional library schools on the continent, in England, and in America." Tai deduced from his findings the subject matter which should determine the content of library education programs and formulated his proposal. Besides being important as the first systematic treatment of professional library education, Tai's interpretations of the social, educational, and intellectual forces that produced libraries and shaped their character are of particular interest and value as a contribution to the development of education for librarianship before 1925.

Training for Librarianship before 1923, also a Ph.D. dissertation, was written by Sarah K. Vann and published in 1961. Vann's purpose was "to view more extensively the events leading to the establishment of the first School of Library Economy, and the activities, both of individuals and the American Library Association," as they related to training between 1887 and 1923.[11] Although limited to library education in the United States, the study assumed classic proportions because of the numerous persons, events, and activities it recorded. Vann's personal interviews with the late Charles C. Williamson and Phineas L. Windsor undoubtedly enhanced the significance of her study. The real contribution of her work, however, lay in the several research problems which she suggested through her many discussions of persons, events, and activities relating to the development of education for librarianship.

The Origin of the American Library School by Carl M. White, also published in 1961, was the product of the author's efforts to understand "how the American library school originated and how its main lines of policy and organization as of the 1920's came to be sculptured as they were."[12] While covering essentially the same period as Vann, White was more selective in recording incidents relating to library education. Concentrating only on meaningful social changes and ideas that contributed to the concept of systematic professional education, he showed that the American library school was an outgrowth of this concept. White's fresh interpretations of the seminal ideas and creative actions which contributed to the evolution of the library school between 1850 and 1920 are of primary importance to students of education for librarianship.

An essay by Louis R. Wilson, "Historical Development of Education for Librarianship in the United States," was not a history, and was not meant to be one. In it the author briefly discussed what he considered "the most important movements, events, and influences that . . . characterized the development" of education for librarianship.[13] Beginning with the establishment of the School of Library Economy at Columbia in 1887, Wilson focused attention on ten factors that greatly influenced the development of library education up to 1948. This essay contributed greatly to the idea for the present study.

The purpose of this study is to analyze and explain the "movements, events, and influences" that made distinctive contributions to the development of education for librarianship between 1919 and 1939. While several investigations have been made of specific aspects of education for librarianship during this period, no systematic study of the kind attempted here has been made.

The basic propositions of the study are: (1) that the status of education for librarianship in 1939 was the product of interactions between traditional concepts of library education and emerging new forces; and (2) that the failure to develop an acceptable system of library education was due to the absence of a unifying force and to attempts to satisfy the competing and specialized needs of librarianship.

Of the movements and events recorded here, the following are given special consideration: (1) the proposals of Charles C. Williamson, Emma Baldwin, and Ernest J. Reece; and (2) the origin and activities of the Committee on Library Training, the Professional Training Section, the Association of American Library Schools, the Committee on Certification and Standardization, the Library Workers' Association, the Board of Education for Librarianship, and the Carnegie Corporation's Ten-Year Program in Library Service. Some effects of the specialization of librarianship, the Great Depression, and the regional accrediting agencies are also considered.

The students, faculties, financial support, and curricula of library schools are treated only incidentally in this study. This is not because they are unimportant aspects of the development of library education, but rather because of the necessity to limit the study. Furthermore, these aspects have already been the subjects of several studies, the most notable of which are: *Training for Library Service* by Charles C. Williamson; *Pre-Professional Backgrounds of Students in a Library School* by Eugene H. Wilson; *Characteristics of the Graduates of the University of California School of Librarianship* by J. Periam Danton and LeRoy C. Merritt; "The American Library School Today," by Louis R. Wilson; *The Curriculum in Library Schools* by Ernest J. Reece; *Programs for Library Schools* by Ernest J. Reece; *The Program of Instruction in Library Schools* by Keyes D. Metcalf, John D. Russell, and Andrew D. Osborn; *Education for Librarianship* by J. Periam Danton; *Progress and Problems in Education for Librarianship* by Joseph L. Wheeler; and finally, the most comprehensive data on the topics—students, faculties, finances, and curricula—are those collected and analyzed by Robert D. Leigh for the Public Library Inquiry, and reported in Part 4 of *The Public Library* by Alice I. Bryan.

This study is a history and the details included in it have been derived from a critical survey of historical documents. Besides the numerous special reports, scholarly investigations, speeches, editorials, factual articles, and books—all of which are documented in the study—the following documents have been critically examined and used: addresses and proceedings of the National

Education Association; annual and special reports of the Board of Education for Librarianship; annual and special reports of the Carnegie Corporation as well as published statements by officers of the corporation; annual and special reports of the Temporary Library Training Board; annual reports of the Committee on Library Training; bulletins and annual reports of library schools; minutes and proceedings of the Association of American Library Schools; minutes of the Council and Executive Board of the American Library Association; papers and proceedings of the American Library Institute; proceedings of the Association of American Universities; proceedings of the Association of Colleges and Secondary Schools of the Southern States; proceedings of the North Central Association of Colleges and Secondary Schools; proceedings of the Special Libraries Association; reports of the Library Workers' Association; reports of the Special Committee on Certification, Standardization, and Library Training; *School Library Yearbook* of the American Library Association Education Committee; and transactions and proceedings of the National Association of State Universities.

The findings and conclusions of a historical investigation are debatable, not only because of possible faulty judgment but also because of unavoidable incompleteness of sources. An obvious limitation has been placed on this investigation by the absence of manuscript sources. However, because of the many published speeches and reports of leading library educators and library school administrators which appeared during the period 1919–39, the findings and conclusions of this study are likely to withstand the most rigorous scrutiny.

2. The Temporary Library Training Board

After the end of World War I, members of the American Library Association plunged into a series of activities which revitalized librarianship and which focused attention on some of its acute problems, one of which was education for librarianship. This chapter includes a description of the association's source of vitality and leadership after the war and a description of how the inadequacies of education for librarianship were revealed and discussed. The origins of movements and proposals relating to the improvement of library education are also identified, analyzed, and explained.

The American Library Association convened its forty-first annual meeting at Asbury Park, New Jersey, June 23–27, 1919. This assembly was in some significant respects unlike any of the association's previous conventions. It was the first postwar convention and those in attendance were not the usual delegates who gathered annually to hear uneventful addresses, reports, and resolutions. On the contrary, these were librarians who, in the words of the president of the association, had "dreamed dreams and seen visions" and had organized and worked to make them realities;[1] these were librarians who were meeting for the first time after having been on the battle-fields and in the reading rooms which were established in barracks at home and overseas; these were librarians who felt they had gained, because of their unique contribution to the war, "a professional status in the minds of thousands of commanding officers, soldiers, sailors, and marines," many of whom were now also returning to civilian life. These were, in short, librarians who had gained experience and confidence through their highly successful Library War Service Program, and who were sure they could not, at this convention, review the past nor discuss the future "in exactly the same spirit as of old."[2] The success of the Library War Service Program had made this highly unlikely.

The Library War Service Program came into existence when the American Library Association accepted the invitation from the War Department's Commission on Training Camp Activities "to take charge of the work of providing reading matter for soldiers, not only by securing books and distributing them, but also by providing library buildings and librarians."[3] The association accepted the invitation not only because there was a "distinct feeling" that all military and civilian personnel should be provided as many opportunities for recreation and self-improvement as possible, but also because the government was asking librarians to "render service along strictly professional lines," just as it was asking doctors and chemists to serve as doctors and chemists.[4] Given this recognition and opportunity, the association organized and put into action a library service program which surpassed all its expectations. Initially, the association hoped to serve at least 1 million men, but in less than a year it had already served 2.25 million, and by November 11, 1919, some library service had been extended to more than 4 million men of the Army, Navy, and Marine Corps.[5] In order to finance this program and to secure reading materials and personnel, the association appealed to the American public for help.

Fortunately, the public's response was quick and generous. During the first eighteen months of the program—from June, 1917, to December, 1918—the association raised 6 million dollars; collected 4 million books; and recruited 717 librarians to work at headquarters, military camps, and dispatch offices at home and overseas.[6] These proud contributions of the association toward winning the war were skillfully planned and executed. The convention, therefore, opened on a jubilant note, having in attendance many of the leaders these formidable tasks had produced. Thus, it was natural for the delegates to direct their attention and energy to the many problems which were plaguing librarianship, not the least of which was education for librarianship.

LIBRARY NEEDS OF THE POSTWAR ERA

From 1887 to about 1919, education for librarianship was theoretically a concern of the American Library Association, but its activities in this area were governed more by tradition and caution than by boldness and improvements. Hence, active efforts to improve the quality of library education and to expand opportunities for professional training became the primary concern of first, the Committee on Library Training; then, the Section on Professional Training for Librarianship; and finally, the Association of American Library Schools.

As a gesture of its desire to become more aware of what was occurring in the area of library education, the American Library Association created, in 1903, the Committee on Library Training and authorized it "to investigate from time to time the whole subject of library schools and courses of study, and report the results of its investigations, with recommendations," to the association.[7] This was a praiseworthy action which never fully materialized, mainly because the association failed to provide adequate financial support. Because of its own inadequacies, because the questions of library education were so pervasive, and because the desire for consultation among the library schools was so great, the Committee on Library Training recommended the establishment of a "normal section of the Association" which would deal with all phases of preparation for librarianship.[8] Subsequently, the Council of the American Library Association established, in 1909, the Section on Professional Training for Librarianship to serve as a forum for the discussion of questions pertaining to the preparation and qualification for librarianship.[9]

It may have been possible to discuss all questions pertaining to the training of librarians in the Section on Professional Training for Librarianship, but some library school teachers and administrators felt that this would be undesirable and that discussions of "distinctly internal school problems of much interest to schools, but of little concern to others" were needed; consequently,

a conference of library school faculties was held in Chicago, January 5, 1911. . . . Sixteen representatives from nine schools were present, and the meeting was entirely unofficial and informal. A list of topics for discussion had been sent out with the call for the meeting and in general these topics were of a sort not likely to find a place in the program of the Professional Training Section. The discussions were felt to be so profitable that a similar meeting was arranged for the following winter in Chicago.[10]

In January, 1915, after four such meetings, the group voted to organize the Association of American Library Schools. Any library school could join the ten chartered members by requiring for admission four years of high school or its equivalent, by offering at least one full year of training, by preparing students for general library work rather than for specific positions, by having a faculty of at least two full-time teachers, and by evidencing adequate financial support and a sound curriculum.[11] In the absence of an official accrediting agency, membership in the association was tantamount to becoming an accredited library school.

These groups—the Committee on Library Training, the Professional Training Section, and the Association of American Library Schools—all had as their chief objective the improvement of library education. The intensity with which they pursued their objective had not been diminished by the war. On the contrary, a new burst of energy was released at this first postwar meeting and they began to explore the idea that not only more and better-trained librarians were going to be demanded, but also that more librarians were going to be trained for specific kinds of libraries, such as schools, businesses, industries, colleges, and universities. They began to question critically whether the traditional concept of one library education curriculum for all types of librarians was still suitable. Appropriately enough, these exchanges of facts and opinion took place during the first postwar program of the Professional Training Section.

A basic assumption of those who planned the program of the Section on Professional Training was that education for librarianship, as it existed in 1919, did not meet the varied and dynamic needs of the entire profession. The experimental teaching methods of the colleges, expanding research, and growing research collections of universities were demanding librarians trained in both advanced subject matter and library science. Similarly, the progressive teaching methods of elementary and secondary schools, along with the enactment of laws requiring specific training for school librarians suggested a need for library education programs appropriate to this group of librarians. Likewise, the growing importance of current literature and basic research to the competitive posture of business and industry was requiring persons trained not only in library science, literature, and the humanities, but also psychology, sociology, economics, chemistry, and engineering. Accordingly, the theme of the 1919 meeting of the Professional Training Section was "Library Training along New Lines and Specialized Library Service."[12]

Andrew Keogh, librarian of Yale University, discussed the preprofessional and professional needs of academic librarians.[13] He focused attention on the frustrating plight of (1) the subject specialist who, while working in a college or university library, desired to become better educated through formal training and of (2) the experienced librarian who desired to become a subject specialist. He emphasized that the present library schools were of little help to either person. The subject specialist, having already mastered on the job the library science courses which the library schools offered, wanted graduate work in library science. Conversely, the library school graduate who wanted to become a subject specialist could not readily enter a graduate school because he did not possess the bachelor's degree which had not been required by the library school for matriculation. Consequently, low admission requirements of the library schools and lack of graduate library schools limited the opportunities of training for academic librarianship and increased the shortage of qualified college and university librarians.

The shortage of school librarians was also great and would only increase unless the library schools changed their curricula in such a way as to train more school librarians or to encourage other educational agencies to do so. More and more educators were beginning to realize that "where the librarian is trained 'the library is attributed to be the common center of school interest'; where an already overworked teacher does her best to care for the library, even the need for a library and its place in the school activity fail to be recognized."[14] By 1919, eighteen states had passed laws which required a definite type and quantity of library training for school librarians. Still, the library schools were not making any changes in their curricula in order to meet the demands for more and better-educated school librarians, and, while graduating about 220 school librarians a year, they were being told to "think in terms of hundreds and thousands when planning for high school and other school libraries of the future."[15]

Special libraries, like academic and school libraries, were also short of trained personnel, and for the same reason: library schools refused to educate librarians for the various types of libraries and positions. Therefore, special librarians could only watch apprehensively as library services became increasingly specialized with no apparent notice from the library schools. Departments and divisions of fine arts, business, economics, science, technology, and children's literature were becoming common in the large public libraries. Special libraries for medicine, law, agriculture, business, and industry were likewise becoming more important to researchers, professionals, and businessmen.[16] Nonetheless, in 1919, it was common criticism that library schools were still devoting most of their curricula to the humanities, literature, and the traditional library courses, and too few of them were willing to consider training librarians for the libraries which were serving science, technology, business, and industry.[17]

Thus, this first postwar meeting of the Professional Training Section was used to present and discuss the above problems pertaining to the personnel needs of the various types of libraries and the inability of the library schools and training classes to graduate an adequate number of well-educated and professionally trained librarians. The speakers painted a composite picture which showed American business, industry, and educational institutions responding to the fragmenting forces of specialization. This response was resulting in needs not only for more and better-educated librarians, but also for professionally trained university, college, school, and special librarians. Similarly, the picture depicted library schools and training classes responding more to personnel needs of the past rather than to those of the present and future. However well the library education agencies had prepared librarians in the past, their performance in 1919 was considered inadequate to meet the library personnel needs of business, industry, and education.

WILLIAMSON AND BALDWIN

In the wake of this storm of criticism of library education, individuals and committees followed with their findings and proposals to increase the number of trained librarians and to raise the standards of library education. A special committee of the American Library Institute reported that there were in progress five investigations which were exploring the possibilities of creating university departments, schools, or training courses for carrying library education beyond the points then attempted by the library schools.[18] Included in the five investigations was a "very significant inquiry of the New England College Librarians" which included facts about needs and lack of graduate library training for college librarians.[19] Helpful as these discussions and investigations were in raising the level of concern about the need for improvements in library education, little was actually done before Charles C. Williamson and Emma Baldwin presented their separate and concrete proposals for preparing more librarians and raising the standards of all library education.

Charles C. Williamson, a staff member of the New York Public Library, made his first critical appraisal of American librarianship in 1918.[20] A year later he was asked to identify and analyze the main problems of library education. He reported the results of his study to the American Library Association on June 26, 1919. Williamson observed that library personnel were being trained in library schools, training classes, apprentice classes, and summer programs, and that where standards existed they were too low to expect the graduates of these agencies to be well-educated and professionally trained librarians. He also observed that there was no meaningful coordination between these training agencies, and advised that a person must be a hopeless optimist who could "see in the present training situation anything more than a variety of valuable parts scattered around waiting for vital machinery not yet constructed or even planned."[21]

Williamson was convinced that these valuable parts—library schools, training classes, apprentice classes, and summer schools—could become a coordinated and strong system of library education with high standards only if the American Library Association assumed its duty as the heart of such a system. Consequently, he urged the association to "establish forthwith a training board—an A.L.A. Training Board, analogous to the A.L.A. Publishing Board."[22] The training board, he further advised, should be truly representative, composed of library educators, administrators, and practitioners.

The basic function of the training board, which Williamson envisioned as having a permanent staff of experts, would be to coordinate the training programs of all the library-education agencies and "to work out and adopt a scheme of standards of fitness for all grades of library service and to grant appropriate certificates to properly qualified persons."[23] Such standardizing and accrediting activities by a duly constituted agency of a national organization, Williamson urged, had ample precedent and was being effectively used to raise the standards of general education and professional training in teaching, engineering, law, and medicine. The association's Committee of Library Training, in his estimation, was inadequate to make the changes in the total structure of library education which the rapidly changing state of American librarianship demanded. Only the American Library Association,

Williamson concluded, could create an agency with support and authority to improve education for librarianship.

Emma Baldwin, a member of the staff of the Brooklyn Public Library and a knowledgeable student of the problems of education for librarianship, was asked by the American Library Institute's Committee on the Higher Education of Librarians to prepare a memorandum on ways and means to improve the quality of library education. In her response she outlined a four-point program.[24]

Baldwin, like Williamson, felt the first step should be taken by the American Library Association in the form of leadership and the preparation of a set of standards which would state the minimum requirements for the admission of new librarians into the profession, and which would make a distinction between the clerical and professional aspects of librarianship. Unlike Williamson, however, Baldwin did not believe it was practical to work out a complete scheme of standards for all professional grades at once, but rather to raise the standards of library education by beginning with new librarians and proceeding systematically to all the higher grades.

Next, she suggested that the basic problems of admission requirements, curriculum, and certification of librarians could be solved by aligning library education with teacher education. From her study of the normal schools of New York City, Baldwin observed that they had "already become standardized to a very large extent, "and that librarians could hardly do better than to make requirements for entrance to the library profession similar to those of the teaching profession. She stated, moreover, that normal schools accepted graduates of high schools and required two years of successful study, at the end of which the student received a temporary license to teach in his or her city or state; this was certification that the student had met the minimum requirements for admission to the teaching profession. Further advancements would depend on experience and additional study. Library schools, in contrast, required all candidates for admission to take examinations in general information, literature, and languages, and required only one year of study. Baldwin concluded "that the character of instruction in the normal school was unquestionable quite as exacting and broad in its scope as that of the library school, while the length of the course was in favor of the normal school."[25]

State certification of librarians and the establishment of a graduate library school were Baldwin's third and fourth points.

State certification of librarians, she urged, would give prestige and establish a pattern of standardization at the state level which could serve as a guide for equal salaries for all grades of library training and classes of library work.

Finally, Baldwin reemphasized that her proposals "would be the minimum requirements for entrance into the profession, but facilities for training would by no means cease at the normal school grade," because college, university, and special libraries could best be served by graduates of library schools who had continued to study some specific subject. She felt these libraries did not need librarians who would be seeking greater knowledge of library technique, but rather those wanting to become subject specialists. A graduate library school, therefore, was needed that would "compete favorably with the graduate schools in other professions and render . . . training in bibliographical research and administration of libraries."[26]

Certainly, the unique element of Baldwin's four-point proposal was her suggestion that library schools be aligned with normal schools in order to raise entrance requirements, standardize curricula, and implement state certification of librarians.

THE SPECIAL COMMITTEE ON STANDARDIZATION, CERTIFICATION, AND LIBRARY TRAINING

While the proposals from both Baldwin and Williamson had much to commend them for further consideration, the Executive Board of the American Library Association accepted Williamson's proposal, and after further discussion of it, concluded "that the appropriate time had not arrived for the appointment of an examining board."[27] It authorized, instead, the appointment of the Special Committee on Standardization, Certification, and Library Training. This committee attempted, during the next three years, to define the objectives and duties of the proposed board, to draw up a tentative scheme of certification, and to gain financial support for the recommended board.

The special committee observed, as it worked to establish objectives and duties for the proposed board, that there were already six groups working on problems of library education: the Committee on Library Training, the Professional Training Section, the Association of American Library Schools, the Committee on Standardization of Libraries and Certification of Librarians, the League of Library Commissions, and the Secondary Education and Library Departments of the National Education Association. Likewise, it noted five types of library training agencies: the library schools, training classes, apprentice classes, summer programs, and programs of normal schools. Still, the complaints were loud that entrance requirements were too low, curricula were inadequate, and training agencies were uncoordinated. Nonetheless, the special committee concluded "that the establishment of a board confined to giving professional certification based on examination, library experience or possession of library school diplomas or certificates might obstruct rather than promote professional standards."[28] Instead, it recommended to the Council the following action:

(1) That a National Board of Certification for Librarians be established by the American Library Association . . . (2) That this Board shall investigate all existing agencies for teaching library subjects and methods, shall evaluate their work for purposes of certification, shall seek to correlate these agencies into an organized system . . . and shall establish grades of library service with appropriate certificates. . . . (3) That the creation of such a board shall have as one of its purposes the stimulation . . . of the improvement of library service and the professional status of library workers . . . (4) That, pending constitutional provision for such a board, the Executive Board of the American Library Association be instructed to appoint a special committee of nine members . . . and that adequate financial support for this board be provided from funds procured through the Enlarged Program campaign or otherwise.[29]

The Council of the American Library Association, on June 3, 1920, adopted the second, third, and fourth recommendations and accepted the committee's report.[30] Prior to this action, the association had consistently refused to enter the uncharted areas of certification of librarians and standardization of library education. By this action it changed its course and entered the mainstream of professional educational activities which medicine, law, and theology had entered years earlier and thereby raised the standards of education and performance to higher levels in their respective professions. The association's action was likewise expected to be of fundamental importance to the future development of library education.

The next year, 1921, the second special committee submitted for discussion and criticism a tentative scheme of certification, urging the association to adopt it or some similar scheme. The scheme was new and the special committee was aware of the opposition it would engender. "Honest differences of opinions will naturally arise in working out details, but no discussion of matters of details can be allowed to obscure the objective we have at heart. . . . "[31] This objective was to raise the standards of library education by eventually requiring, through certification, a bachelor's degree plus one year of professional training for all professional librarians, without doing injustice to those already in service and training.[32]

The tentative scheme itself had four main classes—three for professional librarians and one for clerical workers. One's general and professional education, experience and competency determined one's place in the scheme. Where a bachelor's degree or its equivalent and one year of professional training were lacking, successful completion of an examination, experience, and competency were acceptable substitutes. The scheme of certification, therefore, did not bar any qualified person from entrance to librarianship, but it did place a premium on college and library school training.

DEFEAT OF THE TENTATIVE SCHEME OF CERTIFICATION

Apprehensiveness and attacks were engendered by the tentative scheme of certification, on grounds that it was a cure more dangerous than the diseases afflicting library education, and that it was unfair to the more than 10,000 nonlibrary school graduates. The association's Committee on Library Training was the first to alter its position relative to the work of the Special Committee on Certification and Standardization.

The Committee on Library Training had voted earlier to support Williamson's original proposal, and had recommended, pending the establishment of a certification board, "the acceptance of the standards established by the Association of American Library Schools as a basis for accrediting such schools."[33] A year later, in 1921, the committee restated its willingness to cooperate with the Special Committee on Certification, but added that "of course the basis for accrediting the regular library schools would be— as decided by the committee a year ago—the standards established by the Association of American Library Schools," apparently overlooking the point that this had been only a tentative recommendation at its conception.[34] Nonetheless, by this action it granted the power of accrediting the regular library schools to the Association of American Library Schools and withheld endorsement of the tentative scheme of certification presented by the committee with which it had agreed to cooperate very closely.

More direct disapprovals of the tentative scheme of certification were registered, however, by J. H. Friedel and the Library Workers' Association, Friedel, editor of *Special Libraries*, agreed with the supporters of certification that professional librarians were poorly trained and that this contributed to their low esteem and pitiable salaries, but he disagreed with their proposal to use certification to improve the situation. Such a method, he argued, was not only impractical but harmful. Certification would be no cure because it meant putting a stamp of approval on poorly trained librarians from substandard training agencies. It would not touch the roots of the problems. These, Friedel suggested, could only be reached by insisting "that every library and every agency that pretends to train for librarianship conform to approved standards."[35] To do otherwise would be penalizing the individual because he had met the requirements expected of him. "Certification may provide a very pretty means to keep the individual in a strait-jacket, it may provide a very plausible method for continuing to keep salaries as low as they are, but it cannot," Friedel argued, "raise the standards of professional education."[36]

Additional opposition to the tentative scheme of certification was raised by the Library Workers' Association, which was organized in the spring of 1920 to promote the educational and occupational interests of library workers who were not college and library school graduates.[37] Unlike Friedel, the association was not against the principle of certification, but simply opposed to the particular scheme being offered by the Special Committee on Certification.[38] The tentative scheme of certification, the association charged, placed the more than 10,000 nonlibrary school graduates at a disadvantage: as they aspired to higher paying library positions, they would have to take examinations and the library school graduates would not.[39]

Another basic objection to the scheme was that the Library Workers' Association was committed to the preservation of the apprenticeship system of training and the Special Committee on Certification was committed to its discontinuance. The association felt that librarianship should remain open to persons like those of its membership—intelligent and alert persons with broad interests and attractive personalities, but not college graduates. The association argued, moreover, that when such persons were found, regardless of their college or professional training, they should be admitted to the profession and shown the "means by which they may acquire additional formal training and education while engaged in library work."[40]

The above criticisms of the tentative scheme of certification undoubtedly contributed to its defeat, but the most important contributing factor was lack of financial support to implement it. The committee was so convinced that its program could not be carried out without financial backing that it recommended no steps be taken to implement it until an adequate budget was provided. The American Library Association never provided such a budget. Hence, the idea of raising the standards of education for librarianship through certification and standardization, first proposed by Charles C. Williamson in 1919, was defeated in 1923 by effective criticism and a lack of financial support.

POSITIVE ACTION BY THE COMMITTEE ON LIBRARY TRAINING

The Special Committee on Certification and Standardization, while unable to institute a program of certification, made a worthwhile contribution toward the improvement of library education by causing the American Library Association to accept as its duty the job of accrediting library training agencies. Implementation of this new responsibility became a function of the Committee on Library Training.

The Committee on Library Training, by recommending in 1923 that the American Library Association appoint a board "to survey and investigate the field of library training agencies for the purpose of defining standards . . . and promoting education for librarianship in every way," reversed its position which was taken on this question in 1921.[41] At that time, the committee recommended the acceptance of the standards established by the Association of American Library Schools. The committee reversed its position because it had been unable to persuade the library schools to standardize aspects of their curricula and to increase the opportunities for obtaining library training. In its report for 1920–21, the committee submitted to the library schools "as worthy of consideration" the idea of offering correspondence and summer school courses which would count toward a library school degree; of developing a uniform system of evaluating the credits granted by the schools for the various courses in the curricula; and the possibility of offering special library courses in business, law, and agriculture.[42] A year later, 1921–22, the committee submitted these suggestions in the form of specific recommendations to ALA Council.[43] Three of them—that regular library schools offer summer courses for credit toward a degree, that some schools offer correspondence courses, and that a uniform system of credits be adopted—were debated in Council and a decision was reached to refer the recommendations to the Association of American Library Schools.[44]

In preparation for the reversal of its position on the question of who should accredit library training agencies, the Committee on Library Training, in its report for 1923, reviewed the efforts which had been made since 1919 to raise the standards of library education and to increase the opportunities for such training. It noted the work Williamson did in 1919, and the activities of the Special Committees on Certification and Standardization. It also reviewed its own futile efforts to increase the opportunities for getting professional training, and concluded that the time had come for "the American Library Association to exercise a more positive influence over the various library training agencies of the country."[45] It recommended to the Council "that a Temporary Library Training Board be appointed by the Executive Board to investigate the field of library training, to formulate tentative standards for all forms of library training agencies, to devise a plan for accrediting such agencies, and to report to the Council."[46] This recommendation was accepted and the Executive Board appointed the Temporary Library Training Board in April, 1923.

THE TEMPORARY LIBRARY TRAINING BOARD

The Temporary Library Training Board, financed by a $10,000 grant from the Carnegie Corporation, canvassed the published reports of the library training agencies, conducted surveys, held conferences and open meetings in order: (1) to ascertain the facts about the personnel needs of the profession, (2) to get facts about the inadequacies of library education, (3) to obtain assistance from officials of other professions on questions of standardization and accreditation, and (4) to obtain advice for a provisional scheme of classification for library training agencies.

The temporary board's analyses of the published reports and curricula of the eighteen library training agencies which offered at least a one-year program focused attention on the basic, and in many cases, questionable difference between the agencies. These analyses also provided the board with a clearer picture of the problems the profession itself would have to solve before the standards of education for librarianship could be raised.

These problems were discussed at the first open meeting on library education that the temporary board held during the midwinter meetings of January, 1924. The board was seeking suggestions not only from librarians but also information from officials of other professions that had tackled the complexities of standardization and accreditation of professional education.[47] Therefore, invited to these meetings were authorities on professional education from medicine and education as well as members of the Association of American Library Schools, representatives of the various library agencies, and other librarians who were in attendance at the Midwinter meetings.[48]

Dr. N. P. Colwell, secretary of the Council on Medical Education of the American Medical Association, discussed standardization and accreditation of medical education. He drew a parallel between the problems which were facing the temporary board and those which faced the council when it was first formed. He focused attention on the procedures the council adopted and followed in order to standardize medical schools' entrance requirements, curricula, theory and practice, and faculty qualifications. He reminded the librarians that no organization knew better than theirs of the requirements of library service and library education. Subsequently, "where there is no legal body in the country to effect standardization, this work became the duty of the Association having to do with the educational system."[49]

Other topics which the temporary board sought and received suggestions on at this meeting were the content of the basic courses of a first-year library school, of a library training class, of an apprentice class, of courses in a summer program, and of courses in normal schools.[50]

Following this meeting the temporary board drafted a preliminary report containing its findings and recommendations, and sent copies of it "to members of the Council, training agencies, state library commissions, and library organizations affiliated with A.L.A." for their reactions. Revisions of the report were made from the returned copies and a provisional report was drafted and published for general comments and criticisms. Also, and very importantly, the temporary board scheduled a second opening meeting on library education to consider the revised version of the provisional report.

This second meeting, which was held April 15–17, 1924, in New York City, was unprecedented; never before had "any general group of librarians devoted three entire days to the free discussion" of the subject of library education.[51] Besides the practicing librarians who were in attendance, twelve of the eighteen library schools, training classes, apprentice classes, summer sessions, normal schools, teachers' colleges, and correspondence courses were represented. Also attending were the chief officers of the

American Library Association's Professional Training Section, the Education Committee, the Association of American Library Schools, the League of Library Commissions, the Special Library Association, and the Library Department of the National Education Association.[52] Thus "a national gathering . . . conferred for three days on library training problems for the benefit of the Temporary Library Training Board, all members of which were in attendance."[53]

The provisional draft of the temporary board's report, which was the center of discussion at the meetings, included an introduction, findings, recommendations, and appendices. The latter included a scheme of classification of the library schools, training classes, apprentice classes, summer courses, courses in normal schools and teachers' colleges, and correspondence courses. Paradoxically, the appendices, although included in the report simply as general information for the council and proposed permanent board, attracted considerable attention and much of the discussions centered about them.

The suggestions and criticisms made to the temporary board indicate something of the nature and range of the concern of those in attendance about the scheme of classification of library training agencies. It was suggested

> that library schools be grouped by kind, and not classed by grade; that instead of classifying library schools descriptions be given; that training classes be held for six months, not for seven and eight months; that regional training classes be established; that there be a definite relation between the salaries which may be received and the amount of preparation which was required . . .; and that summer library courses were extremely valuable and requirements should not be placed so high as to hamper their effectiveness.[54]

Something of the spirit in which the temporary board accepted these suggestions and criticisms may be gained from the knowledge that the report was received "with large and wide appreciation," and the opportunities to exchange views on library education before the official body authorized to set standards of training "provided the best possible start for the library educational system of the future."[55]

After the three-day conference on library education, the temporary board spent a fourth day considering the diverse views that had been submitted and preparing its final report which was presented to the Council of the American Library Association on

June 30, 1924. The report, like its provisional draft, was divided into four parts: an introduction, findings, recommendations, and appendices. The Council was asked to accept the report and to adopt the recommendations.

The secretary of the association read the findings of the temporary board to the sixty-four members of the Council who met at the annual meeting to hear the report:

(1) That the growing importance of libraries as productive factors in community life and as mediums for the diffusion of knowledge has created a demand for librarians with trained minds of a high order; (2) that the agencies now offering education for librarianship are unable to supply a sufficient number of persons to meet the demands; and especially, to fill positions requiring highly specialized preparation and the qualities of leadership; (3) that existing library schools are inadequately financed; (4) that there exists great variation in entrance requirements, curricula, faculty qualifications, and library facilities in those agencies purporting to offer the same quality of education; (5) that there are no facilities for preparing teachers of library science; (6) that there is evident lack of a uniform nomenclature, as well as of a uniform system of credits such as is generally recognized in collegiate practice; (7) that standards of education have been established by individual agencies, or small groups of agencies, but that, in general, no definite qualifications for library work have been required by the profession at large; (8) that there is not sufficient cooperation among training agencies of different types to secure a correlation of the work given by them; and (9) that there exists no organization within or without the profession which has authority to promote and to evaluate the several grades of education for librarianship.[56]

From these findings the temporary board concluded that there was an "acute need for a permanent official body which shall help library educational agencies to develop their resources and to fulfill satisfactorily their function of meeting . . . the changing needs of library service."[57] And it suggested "such a body would be comparable to the national boards or councils that so effectively are improving education in the professions of law, medicine, and dentistry." It, therefore, recommended "that a permanent Board of Education for Librarianship be created;" and that this board shall:

(a) Study library service and its changing needs and promote the further development of education for librarianship; (b) investigate the extent to which existing agencies meet the needs of the profession; (c) formulate for the approval of the Council minimum standards for library schools, for summer library courses, for courses on school library work in normal schools and teachers' colleges, for training and apprentice classes, for correspondence and extension courses, and for other educational agencies as may arise; (d) classify these agencies in accordance with the standards thus adopted; (e) publish annually a list of the accredited agencies; (f) plan for the correlation of the work offered by the agencies, so that a unified system of education for librarianship may be developed; (g) establish throughout the different agencies a uniform system of credits consistent with collegiate practice; (h) assign to the technical terms used in library education meanings which will promote accurate and uniform application; (i) establish close relations with other bodies having similar purposes; (j) serve in an advisory capacity in regard to grants of funds for library education; (k) serve in any other matters which would fall logically within the functions of the Board; and (l) report annually to the A.L.A. Council on the progress of education for librarianship.[58]

The Council of the American Library Association, at the largest meeting of its history, accepted, by unanimous vote, the report of the Temporary Library Training Board, and adopted its recommendations.[59] The Board of Education for Librarianship "was promptly appointed by the Executive Board and it held its first meeting at Saratoga Springs."[60]

Thus, the wave of concern about the confused state of library education at the end of World War I crested five years later. The Temporary Library Training Board, whose activities led to the creation of the Board of Education for Librarianship, was the result of a group of related and sometimes interacting postwar discussions and proposals on the shortage of trained librarians and the weaknesses of library education. The postwar expansion and the fragmenting forces of specialization revealed an acute shortage of suitably trained librarians and some basic inadequacies of the library training agencies. Interest aroused, individuals and groups began to identify the weaknesses of the training agencies and to describe the kind of training that was needed by school, college, university, and special librarians, but was unavailable to them. The proposals that were submitted by Charles C. Williamson and Emma Baldwin for improving the quality and variety of library training led to the creation of the Special Committee of Certification, and its activities caused the Committee on Library Training, the Association of American Library Schools, the Professional Training Section, and the Library Workers' Association to become deeply concerned about problems of library education. The accumulation and interaction of all these diverse activities culminated in the recommendation from the Committee on Library Training to the American Library Association that a temporary training board be established to investigate the field of library education and to make recommendations for its improvement.

By appointing the Temporary Library Training Board, and by acting upon its recommendation to establish the Board of Education for Librarianship, the American Library Association abandoned its irresolute role in the field of library education and established itself as a potentially powerful force for shaping the course of development of education for librarianship.

3. The Board of Education for Librarianship

By creating the Board of Education for Librarianship and by giving to it comprehensive duties, the American Library Association took a significant step towards consolidating its work in the field of library education and towards "acknowledging its responsibility to library training."[1] All of the association's activities regarding library education would now be carried out by this board; the Committee on Library Training and the Committee on National Certification and Library Training, both of which had been appointed by the association, were to be discontinued.[2]

The association, however, was not only concerned with consolidating its efforts, but also with becoming the only spokesman in the field of library education. It underscored this by accepting the conclusion that there was no organization which had authority to promote and to evaluate the several grades of education for librarianship. Moreover, the president of the association called upon the Association of American Library Schools to acknowledge that no organization was better qualified to determine the personnel needs of the profession than the American Library Association.[3]

Thus, by July 1, 1924, the way was cleared for the Board of Education for Librarianship to chart a course of development of

26

library education. This it did between 1924 and 1930 in several ways: by formulating minimum standards for all library training agencies, by sponsoring a library curriculum study, by sponsoring the writing of seven textbooks in library science, by conducting summer institutes for teachers of library science, by securing financial aid for library school students, and by serving as principal advisor to benefactors of library education.

MINIMUM STANDARDS FOR LIBRARY SCHOOLS

The Board of Education for Librarianship collected data for the minmum standards of library schools and established a consensus for their support by methods similar to those which were used by its predecessor, the Temporary Library Training Board. As a point of departure, the board analyzed the repeated assertion that there was a shortage of well-trained librarians and found that it was not an exaggeration. There was a dearth of well-qualified library leaders, specialists, school librarians, and librarians for small libraries and extension work. The total number of all library school graduates who were engaged in library work in December, 1924, was 4,527. This was slightly more than half the number of librarians the elementary and secondary schools alone would need annually, if standards were to be met.[4] Furthermore, the records of the employment service of the American Library Association showed that it was easy to place educated librarians, but difficult to place the uneducated. About 80 percent of those registered with the employment service and not working had not attended a library school. About 75 percent of the requests from employers for recommendations were for persons who had completed at least one year of library school training, and 25 percent were for persons who also held a bachelor's degree. Finally, most of the library schools reported that the demand for well-qualified librarians far exceeded the supply.[5] Hence, there was indeed a shortage of librarians, but only of those who were well-educated.

The board not only gathered additional facts which further demonstrated the shortage of librarians, it also studied the library schools as they were presented in their publications. This study produced evidence which focused further attention on the wide variations between the schools' organization, administration, instructional staff, library facilities, requirements for admission, content of curriculum, and recognition given on the completion of the work. It found that:

The schools ranged from those connected with public libraries to those which . . . were an integral part of academic institutions; from those offering a two-year curriculum . . . to those offering elective courses . . .; from those requiring college graduation for entrance to those admitting on the basis of competitive examinations for which high school graduates . . . were eligible; from those granting a bachelor's degree to those granting a certificate for the completion of one year of work; and from those granting a second bachelor's degree for two years of work to those granting a second bachelor's degree for one year of work.[6]

This analysis of publications was followed by a two-month tour of the schools, during which time the board conferred with the faculties and officials, inspected facilities and book collections, attended classes, and met with students. Thus, the board saw in operation the strong points as well as the weak points of the library education system. In its summary of these visits, the board stated that there were library schools so poorly organized that only a complete reorganization would remedy the situation. Furthermore, most of the schools had inadequate financial support, faculties, facilities, and collections. It also noted, however, that there were effectively organized schools with good faculties, facilities and collections, and that they were doing commendable work, considering their meager financial support.[7]

Adoption of minimum standards for library schools appeared to be the best solution to the existing problems, and the board formulated these by refining the tentative standards which the Temporary Library Training Board had passed on to it. There was a widespread belief among librarians that four years of liberal education plus one year of professional training constituted the minimum ideal education for the beginning librarian. The Committee on Certification and Standardization gave formal expression to this ideal in 1921. But knowing that something is ideal does not make it immediately possible to realize. Other real factors are sometimes more effective in shaping events and programs and the board was undoubtedly aware of this situation. It knew that low library salaries and the low esteem of librarianship were more powerful forces to be dealt with in the formulation of minimum standards than the desire to have a set of minimum standards based on a bachelor's degree and one year of library training. Its problem, consequently, was to find out what the profession was willing to approve and support as minimum standards for library schools. The board, as it searched for this consensus, isolated the basic issues that had to be dealt with: entrance requirements to library schools; academic institutions to which library schools could be transferred or at which they could be started; library school curricula; degrees to be granted; education of library school teachers.[8]

Before 1924, only two library schools—New York State Library School and the Library School of the University of Illinois—required a bachelor's degree for admission. The other schools required at least a high school diploma and feared a decrease in enrollment if more formal education were required. The board, while feeling "it inadvisable to enforce an entrance requirement of college graduation," also felt a high school diploma was not enough.[9] Thus, it cleared the way for the establishment of one year of college education as a minimum standard for admission by showing that 48 percent of the students enrolled in library schools in 1924 were college graduates, and that only 15 percent had less than one year of college education. The fear of higher standards was further allayed by providing for the admission of exceptional applicants who had had no college preparation.

The desire for academic respectability was an obvious reason for trying to connect library schools with colleges and universities, but a more basic reason was the belief that library schools could not become professional institutions as long as they were affiliated with public libraries. A professional school was committed to teaching fundamental principles that were applicable to the solution of an unlimited number of problems. The existence of a library school in a public library undermined this commitment to universality because libraries conducted library schools mainly to supply their own personnel need. Their particular practices and procedures influenced what was taught, preventing the schools from concentrating on universal principles of library science. Such concentration and teaching, it was argued, could only be done at an academic institution. Academic connections for library schools, therefore, was one of the first issues the board had to work out.

The ideal solution to the problem and the one in keeping with the spirit of professional education was academic connections for all library schools. The board, however, could not obtain this ideal because some of the leading library schools—Library School of the New York Public Library, Library School of the Carnegie Library of Atlanta, St. Louis Library School, and the Library

School of the Los Angeles Public Library—were connected with public libraries and their administrators showed no desire to transfer them to academic institutions. The board found a solution to this tangled issue by (1) dividing the library schools into junior undergraduate, senior undergraduate, graduate, and advanced graduate library schools; and by (2) permitting only the junior undergraduate library schools to be "connected or affiliated with an approved library, college, or university."[10] This compromise, while not entirely palatable, permitted all existing library schools to continue their programs.

In seeking its solution to academic affiliation, the board necessarily dealt with the questionable quality of the library school curriculum. Many librarians as well as educators believed the curriculum contained too much "training class material and not enough that was definitely of college undergraduate or graduate level."[11] The board was also of this opinion but did not know what materials should or should not constitute the curriculum. Hence, it drew up only suggestive curricula for the minimum standards and stated it would make appropriate recommendations to the Council of the American Library Association after the completion of its projected analysis of library work.

The problem of the types of certificates and degrees to be granted after the completion of the different levels of library school training—like the issues of the entrance requirements, academic affiliation, and curricula—did not yield to an easy and satisfactory solution. For six years the Association of American Library Schools had unsuccessfully tried to standardize library-education degrees and, as already mentioned, the board found wide variations of practice in this field.[12] That it was highly desirable to standardize degrees as part of the minimum standards was an opinion shared by both the board and the American Association of Library Schools. Consequently, both tacitly agreeing to accept the ruling, the board appealed to the Association of American Universities for a decision on the matter.

The Committee on Academic and Professional Degrees of the Association of American Universities, after studying the curricula and degrees of the library schools, informed the board that the degrees of Bachelor of Library Science and Master of Library Science were undesirable, and that the "degrees of A.B. or B.S. and M.D. or M.S., with or without qualifying phrases 'in library science,' were to be recommended provisionally until work" had been placed on a graduate level.[13] It further informed the board that "the bachelor's degree should be granted only on the basis of usual collegiate standards, including a major of approximately one year in library science." And that "two years should be required for a master's degree. The first year should include vocational courses or equivalent in practice, and lead to a certificate. This certificate and a B.A. or A.B. should be required for admission to candidacy for the master's degree." While these recommendations on academic degrees did not solve all the problems regarding them, they nonetheless allowed the board to construct "minimum standards for all types of library schools with full knowledge of the extent to which they conformed to acceptable collegiate practice."[14]

A shortage of qualified library school teachers loomed large as the final issue requiring a solution before the minimum standards for library schools could be completed. A bachelor's degree, one year of professional training, and some practical knowledge of library science were set as minimum requirements for teachers of junior and senior library schools. Minimum qualifications for teachers in graduate library schools were a bachelor's degree, two years' professional training, practical experience, and any other requirements governing the graduate college of a university. Not all library school teachers met these qualifications, but the board reached agreement on them by adding three provisos. First, it provided for just recognition of competent teachers who did not meet the formal educational requirements; second, it urged the establishment of summer institutes for teachers of library science at a university; and third, it gave the library schools two years to comply with the instructional staff aspect of the minimum standards.

Thus, with agreements obtained on these problems—entrance requirements, academic affiliation of library schools, library schools curricula, degrees to be conferred, and qualifications of faculties—the board completed the details of the minimum standards and submitted them to the American Library Association Council, which adopted them on July 1, 1925.[15] The first published list of accredited library schools appeared a year later.

MINIMUM STANDARDS FOR LIBRARY TRAINING AGENCIES

The minimum standards for library schools left untouched the summer programs in library science, library courses in normal schools, apprentice classes, and training classes that together made up a larger and more heterogeneous group of training agencies than the library schools. No one knew how many of these agencies existed. The defunct Committee on Library Training had reported that it was impossible to obtain meaningful results about library programs in normal schools; that there were thirteen summer programs and the number was increasing; and finally, that at least fifty libraries were offering library training.[16] Likewise, it was a common belief that more librarians were trained outside of the library schools than in them, and that the "overwhelming majority" were trained in apprentice and training classes.[17]

By 1925, however, some libraries had discontinued their training and apprentice classes because of a lack of applicants and need, and others had done so because "it was more satisfactory and less expensive to employ library school graduates than to train apprentices."[18] Still, the board had to complete minimum standards for these agencies before it could organize the different levels of training into a system of library education. This task proved less difficult than at first suspected since the substance of the agreements that had been reached during the formulation of minimum standards for library schools was found to be also applicable to standards for summer courses, apprentice and training classes, and courses for school library work.

Summer Courses in Library Science

Summer courses in library science were offered by the accredited library schools for the professional library degree; by non-accredited institutions which gave essentially the same courses for a certificate; by normal schools, colleges, and universities as part of an academic curriculum for a bachelor's degree; and finally, they were sponsored by library extension agencies. The board did not intend, while standardizing them, to eliminate any of these summer programs. On the contrary, it wanted to increase them and raise their standards of training.[19]

The board classified the accredited and nonaccredited library schools that offered summer courses as types I and II, respectively, and recommended that they "be governed by the same Minimum Standards for Library Schools."[20] Likewise, it classified the normal schools, colleges, and universities as type III and recommended that they be governed by the standards adopted for the junior undergraduate library schools. Finally, it classified as type IV those summer courses that the Library Commission sponsored.

A high school diploma, an aptitude for library work, and a confirmed appointment to a library position were the admission requirements for the type IV summer courses, which contents were to be limited to specific problems of the small libraries.

Despite their limitations and low standards, the board believed these courses necessary because they offered a realistic and practical solution to the shortage of trained librarians for "the small and medium-sized library where limitations of salary, resources, or location . . . made attendance at undergraduate library schools impossible in most cases."[21] The board presented the above minimum standards for summer courses in library science to the Council on January 1, 1926, which adopted them after a few clarifications.[22]

Training and Apprentice Classes

Apprentice classes and training classes, although the oldest training agencies, were not clearly defined as to purpose and scope in 1924. Such a definition was necessary, however, before the board could formulate standards of training. Therefore, it appointed a subcommittee to study the work of these agencies with a view towards defining and standardizing their programs. With the help of the newly organized training class section of the American Library Association, the subcommittee formulated and the board accepted the following definitions of apprentice and training classes:

> *Training Class*—A regularly organized class conducted for a definite period of time for the purpose of supplying the profession at large. Entrance to the class is gained by competitive examinations in cultural subjects, but graduates of academic colleges and universities may be accepted without examination. A 'training class' implies a classroom with desks, equipment, textbooks, and a standardized library for a laboratory. More than fifty per cent of the time of the class is devoted to formal instruction, with problems, on all branches of elementary library science. Examinations are given on the material included in the course of study.
>
> *Apprentice Class*—A few students received at one time and required to do the actual work of the library under supervision of department heads or other experienced workers. The formal instruction is much less in amount than is this practical work and is based entirely on local procedure. All the students may or may not learn all processes and there may or may not be an entrance examination and a final test.[23]

Acceptance of the above definitions enabled the board to formulate minimum standards for apprentice and training classes with the realization that its power to obtain compliance was limited since these were training agencies operated by and for the benefit of the libraries supporting them. The chief elements of the standards that were adopted on March 7, 1926, were: (1) that the class should be conducted by a library that the board had approved for such work; (2) that the class should have at least one full-time teacher; (3) that the full-time teacher should be a college and library school graduate; (4) that the entrance requirements should be a high school diploma and examinations; and (5) that the curriculum should be at least six months' long and a certificate granted for its completion.[24]

Curricula in School Library Work

The final minimum standards formulated and adopted were those for a curriculum in school library work; two sets of standards were formulated to cover these curricula. One set was essentially the same as the standards that had been adopted for the senior undergraduate and graduate library schools, differing mainly in the larger number of courses suggested for school library work. The other set of standards applied to courses in school library work that were being offered at normal schools, colleges, and universities. It included only statements on organization, administration, and the instructional staff, undoubtedly because the board had little definite information about the library science courses that were being offered by normal schools, colleges, and universities. The Council, nonetheless, adopted the standards for a curriculum in school library work on October 8, 1926.[25]

Thus, two years after its creation, the board had formulated and the Council had adopted minimum standards for all library training agencies: library schools, summer programs, apprentice classes, training classes, and curricula for school library work. In formulating these standards, the board had asked for and received advice from officials and authorities of professional education in medicine, law, dentistry, and higher education. Through letters, private conferences, public statements, and open meetings, it likewise had obtained the valuable contributions of librarians who were interested in standardizing and raising the level of education for librarianship. While standards were not ideal, they were what the profession was willing to support at the time.

SUMMER INSTITUTES, CURRICULUM STUDY, AND LIBRARY SCIENCE TEXTBOOKS

A shortage of qualified library science teachers, a lack of knowledge about the content of the library school curriculum, and the absence of library science textbooks were three problems the board had set out to solve even before the minimum standards were adopted. Attention had been focused on the gravity of these problems by the critical study of Charles C. Williamson who found that 48 percent of the library science teachers who gave ten or more lectures in 1921 were not college graduates, and only 7 percent had had training in the art of teaching.[26] No library school, moreover, had attempted to disregard what had "been done in the past and made a thorough, scientific analysis of what training for professional library work should be and build its curriculum upon its findings."[27] Concerning textbooks, Williamson found that virtually none were available for the library training agencies.[28]

In order to prepare more and better-qualified library science teachers, to construct a realistic library science curriculum, and to provide data for library science textbooks, the board launched a three-point program. This included the establishment of summer institutes for library science teachers, the solicitation of funds to conduct a curriculum study, and the selection of librarians to write library science textbooks based on data gathered from the curriculum study.

The first summer institute for library science teachers was held at the University of Chicago in 1926. It was attended by thirty-two students who "represented various library interests, including faculty members from leading library schools and also those with limited teaching experience but years of library work."[29] The second and last such institute was held at the same university a year later.[30] Although there were mixed feelings about the effectiveness of the institutes, they apparently helped some library science teachers to meet the qualifications specified in the minimum standards: the board reported, in 1927, that the faculties of all the accredited library schools connected with colleges and universities were of professional rank.[31] However, despite the probable success of the institutes, the board urged the graduate library schools to assume responsibility for preparing qualified library science teachers and not to leave this important task to summer institutes.

The board began the curriculum study in the fall of 1927. It selected as director Dr. W. W. Charters, an authority on methods of teaching and curriculum construction.[32] He was assisted by two experienced librarians, Harold F. Brigham and Anita M. Hostetter, and an appointed advisory committee of nine persons who represented "the library schools and the outstanding movements in the library world."* The purpose of the study was "to develop through job analysis a complete range of the activities and traits involved in all phases of library work," thereby providing a scientific basis for the construction of a curriculum for library schools and for the writing of library science textbooks.[33]

In order to explain the techniques of job analysis that would be used in the curriculum study, Dr. Charters discussed the six steps taken to obtain the data for the textbook on circulation.[34] First, the duties of the circulation librarian were collected by searching the literature and interviewing librarians. Second, methods of performing circulation duties were collected by searching the literature, interviewing circulation librarians, and observing a selected group of circulation departments of fifty-five libraries, recording on specifically prepared forms "the methods used in each library with all the common practices and variation." Third, analyses and tabulations were made of the collected data. Fourth, the traits of a good circulation librarian were collected by "interviewing librarians, heads of circulation departments, and patrons of libraries." Fifth, Jennie Flexner, the librarian chosen to write the book, began writing by using the collected data as her sources. Sixth, and finally, the first draft of the book "was mimeographed and sent to the library schools to be tried under practice teaching conditions," with the understanding that it would be revised in light of the suggestions and criticisms received; it would then be published.

Dr. Charters, in concluding, assured librarians that the use of job analysis for constructing curricula and writing textbooks was "not startlingly new," but one of the most common and valid methods known. The board endorsed the procedure and recommended that the curriculum study be continued until all the subjects had been analyzed and textbooks had been prepared. Its recommendation was accepted and by 1930 the study was completed and seven textbooks on library science had been published.†

---

*The members of the advisory committee were: Herbert Hirshberg, W. O. Carson, Chalmers Hadley, Elizabeth Kapp, Sydney Mitchell, Rebecca Rankin, Alice Tyler, Harriet Wood, and James Wyer.

†The books in the series were: *Circulation Work in Public Libraries*, by Jennie Flexner; *Reference Work*, by James Wyer; *Introduction to Cataloging and the Classification of Books*, by Margaret Mann; *Library in the School*, by Lucile Fargo; *Book Selection and Order Work for Libraries*, by F. K. W. Drury; and *Library Service for Children*, by Effie Power.

SURVEYS, SCHOLARSHIPS, AND ADVICE

The formulation of minimum standards for all library training agencies, the sponsoring of the curriculum study, and the writing of library science textbooks were not the board's only major accomplishments that gave direction to library education between 1923 and 1930. Its investigations of the personnel needs of all types of libraries; its solicitation of financial aid for library science students; and its advice, especially to benefactors of library education, were also important and influential.

In its first survey of the personnel needs of the profession, the board reported a shortage of library leaders, library specialists, librarians for small libraries and extension work, and children and school librarians. Four years later, the board again reported that "the dearth of candidates for many library positions was evident before the board was created, and is still an acute problem."[35] Yet, in 1929, the board was receiving reports that there was an oversupply of librarians and that if the schools continued to increase and to prepare librarians, the effect would be to reduce salaries.[36] Because of these conflicting claims, the board considered it its obligation to clarify the issues by obtaining more facts about the personnel needs of the profession. Although it did not obtain complete returns from its survey of all geographical regions, the board was still able to conclude from the data it did receive that there was not an oversupply of librarians with special traning and leadership qualities; but rather that "Catalogers, children's librarians, county librarians, school librarians, teachers of library science, executives for public and college libraries, and librarians with an expert knowledge of certain subjects" were in demand.[37] The board further concluded that even though the great depression did "create an unusual supply of unemployed librarians," those affected most were librarians who had received only a general library training. It seemed possible that library schools had not responded promptly enough to the board's suggestions that more specialized training be included in their curricula. Therefore, the board continued to promote education for librarianship by encouraging the establishment of new training agencies wherever there was adequate financial support and a need existed in the region for a library school. It urged this despite the ominous effects of the depression and the rumblings of discontent from the profession, which would eventually force it to reverse its policy.

Before the creation of the board, there was very little financial aid for library science students. The board stated in its first report that "in practically all other professions scholarships and fellowships are available, but there are few in the library profession." Hence, the promotion of library education by providing library science students with financial assistance became part of the board's total program. By the end of 1930, it had secured statements from more than fifty scholarship, fellowship, and loan-fund committees that library science would be considered a subject within the scope of their awards.[38]

To serve, finally, in an advisory capacity in regard to grants and funds for library education was a primary duty assigned to the board when it was created. During its first six years of operation, the board grew to be not only the association's official advisor in regard to funds for library education, but in all matters relating to library education. Colleges and universities planning courses in library science "repeatedly turned to the Board for detailed criticism of curricula, advice on faculty, equipment, quarters and finances."[39]

Similarly, the board's advice was sought and respected by foundations and corporations contemplating gifts for the promotion of library education. The Rockefeller Foundation, the General Education Board, the Rosenwald Fund, and the Carnegie Corporation all gave money to advance library education. The Carnegie Corporation, however, was by far the chief benefactor, and the board was its principal advisor in regard to these grants. For library education alone, this corporation pledged, between 1925 and 1930, more than three million dollars. A special subcommittee could not find a single instance where the corporation made a grant without the advice of the board.[40] Consequently, as principal advisor of benefactors, and especially of the Carnegie Corporation, the board possessed enormous power to direct the course of development of library education before the beginning of the great depression.

THE GREAT DEPRESSION

The economic crisis of the great 1929 depression spread ruin throughout the country and the population. Librarians began to join the ranks of the unemployed when the decline in state and local revenues necessitated a reduction of library staffs, especially in public libraries.[41] At first, only new library school graduates and librarians without any special training were affected,[42] but as the economic crisis deepened, librarians of all grades, training, and experience were affected and were unable to find positions.[43]

In 1932, there were between 15,000 and 18,000 trained librarians with about 1,500 or 1,600 joining the profession annually.[44] A survey of 227 representative libraries and 21 state extension agencies showed that in 1933 there were 1,044 professionally trained librarians who were unemployed.[45] The American Library Association Subcommittee on Unemployment reported, later in 1933, that there were 3½ times as many unemployed library school graduates (1,590) in September, 1933, as there were in December, 1931, when there were only 444.[46] But the increase in unemployment of professional librarians had reached its peak by the end of 1933. In 1934, there were 560 more librarians employed than the year before, and this number did not include new library school graduates who were also able to find work.[47] Moreover, the decrease in unemployment continued, and by January, 1937, the employment opportunities had improved so greatly that the A.L.A. Subcommittee on Unemployment felt that there was no longer any need to make an annual report on the subject.[48] Hence, the severe unemployment that was caused among professional librarians by the economic crisis of the depression was ended by 1938. However, during the crisis, the course of the development of library education as it had been outlined by the Board of Education for Librarianship had been changed.

On the eve of the great depression, the board had committed itself to an expansion program in library education, particularly in the area of the school librarian programs. Not only had the board completed standards for school library curricula in teachers colleges, but it was also supporting the rationale for establishing such programs.[49] Furthermore, it was actively encouraging the establishment of new library schools, especially in those sections of the country where there were no training agencies.[50] Likewise, it was trying to persuade the accredited library schools to offer more specialized library training.[51]

Thus, when the critics of the board gave their first warning concerning the oversupply of librarians, the board did not admit that such was entirely the case. Rather, as stated earlier, it replied that there was not an oversupply of specially trained librarians.[52]

The board's correct assessment of the problem at the time, however, did not silence its critics who had gone a step further by stating that the oversupply of librarians was caused by the board's library education expansion policy.[53]

Unfortunately, because of the large number of inferior school librarian curricula that were being started in teachers colleges in order to meet the demands for school librarians, the board was especially vulnerable, even though its actions were not the cause of the rapid development of these programs. Indeed, the board was as concerned about the rapid spread of inferior school librarian programs as its critics.[54]

Nonetheless, as the effects of the depression began to reach not just librarians who were new graduates and generalists only, but also those who had special training plus years of experience, the board found it impossible to defend its expansion program. Therefore, in 1932, it capitulated to the combined forces of criticism and unemployment and called a halt to its program by asking the accredited library schools to reduce their enrollments.[55] And later, "through its advisory service and recommendations to the Carnegie Corporation of New York on grants to library schools, the Board discouraged the establishment of new professional courses in librarianship."[56]

The Association of American Library Schools actively encouraged and fully supported these actions of the board.[57] This was unfortunate because it placed the board in the position of joining the association in focusing attention on the allegation that unemployment among librarians was due primarily to an oversupply of library school graduates—a situation made progressively worse by the large number of librarians trained in the summer programs and teachers colleges. The Association of American Library Schools and many of its members, even before 1932, supported this point of view and they were later joined by the American Library Association Junior Members Round Table.[58]

It was quite true that a very large percentage of the unemployed librarians were recent library school graduates and that the enrollments of the accredited library schools were still high in 1932.[59] It was likewise true that a large number of librarians and teacher-librarians were being prepared by the teachers colleges, and that these, plus those from the accredited library schools, aggravated the unemployment situation. However, it was a mistake to stress excess of librarians as a primary cause of unemployment among librarians. The unusually high rate of unemployment among librarians, like that among all other groups in America between 1929–39, was due primarily to the economic crisis caused by the great depression. To argue otherwise, one had to ignore the great demand for trained librarians that was created by both the regional accrediting agencies and by the extension of library service to business and industry. Moreover, unemployment among librarians dropped in proportion to the economic recovery of the country.

The consequences of this mistake were grave because they led to a reduction in the number of librarians trained by accredited library schools,[60] while there appears no evidence that they also reduced the number of those librarians and teacher-librarians who were supposedly receiving inadequate training through inferior library education programs offered by the teachers colleges. Furthermore, and probably more importantly, the reduction in library school enrollment resulted in a reduction in the number of trained librarians at a time when a third of the country had no local library facilities, and another third was inadequately served.[61] But despite the fact that only a third of the country's population was receiving adequate library service from trained librarians, the board did not return to the boldness that characterized its expansion program in library education before 1929, and that was probably needed in 1939.

Thus, the creation, in 1924, of the Board of Education for Librarianship led to a decade of improvement. The newly created board had been given authority over and responsibility for both the quality and quantity of library education that was to be provided. The board had planned and was carrying out a series of significant programs toward fulfilling its purpose when the depression caused a curtailment of its activities. Between 1924 and 1934, the board formulated and the association approved minimum standards for all library training agencies; it sponsored institutes for library school teachers and the writing of a series of library science textbooks; and it promoted the advancement of library education by identifying and publicizing the special training that librarians needed, by encouraging the wise establishment of library training agencies, and by serving as advisor to the benefactors of library education.

But the board's improvement programs were brought to a grinding halt in 1932 by the high rate of unemployment caused by the depression. Although the peak of unemployment by librarians was over by 1934 and employment opportunities greatly improved by 1937, the board never regained the vigor that had characterized it before the great depression.

4. The Carnegie Corporation's Ten-Year Program

By creating the Board of Education for Librarianship in 1924, the American Library Association assumed responsibility for establishing standards for professional library education and for certifying those agencies providing it. This was a clear departure from its role before 1924, and the substantial power and comprehensive duties it gave the board created an enormous potential for improving the quality of library education. The degree to which this potential became a reality was due mainly to the financial support both the association and the board received from the Carnegie Corporation through its Ten-Year Program in Library Service which began in 1926.

In 1925, Frederick P. Keppel, president of the Carnegie Corporation, submitted a proposed program in library service to the trustees of the corporation. In this proposal he stated that the time had come for the corporation to adopt a program in library service that would continue the corporation's special interests in this field, and that would, at the same time, provide for the endowment of library schools and library organizations.[1] The decision to submit this proposed program was based on two influential library surveys, the work of the Temporary Library Training Board and the Board of Education for Librarianship. The first survey was made by Alvin S. Johnson in 1917, and the second by Charles C. Williamson in 1921.

THE JOHNSON REPORT

In 1914, it became clear to the trustees of the Carnegie Corporation that many cities which had received Carnegie funds to assist them in building public libraries were not keeping their financial pledges. Two years later the trustees concluded that a study of the corporation's "wide provision of public library buildings" was needed, and it engaged Dr. Alvin S. Johnson, director of the New School for Social Research, to make the study.

In part, the trustees asked Dr. Johnson "to estimate as far as possible the value of the social forces which have to do with the creation of the library in a community;" and "to determine whether these social forces are quickened or are rendered less active by outside aid;" and further "to inquire into the library schools and to report on the adequacy of their output of trained librarians."[2]

A year later, 1917, Dr. Johnson submitted to the trustees his final report: "A Report to the Carnegie Corporation of New York on the Donation to Free Public Libraries." Its findings "covered matters of personnel, facilities, and training, and provided a new basis for the operation of the Corporation" with regard to library service.[3] However, World War I, which America entered three months after the appearance of Dr. Johnson's report, placed immediate demands on money, materials, and manpower, thereby interrupting the corporation's plans for promoting education through a new approach to helping libraries.

In addition to delaying the corporation's new plan, the war caused the corporation to adopt two positive wartime measures regarding library service and library buildings. First, it agreed to help the association with its Library War Service Program by helping "to erect, stock, and administer thirty-two army cantonments library buildings. [Second] to end immediately its policy of making grants for free public library buildings, no matter how anxious communities might be to have buildings."[4]

These wartime delays and decisions gave the corporation time to consult with the library profession about the present and future needs of library service. It found that "the question of training librarians was an urgent one—and one to which Mr. Carnegie had been almost impervious—and by March 18, 1918, the Corporation had in mind to set up a study of the schools for the training of librarians."[5] A year later, Dr. Charles C. Williamson was engaged to make this study.

THE WILLIAMSON REPORT

Dr. Charles C. Williamson, although not a professionally educated librarian, was one of the most astute observers of the library situation in America, and of library education in particular. Before being invited to survey the library schools, he had been the head of the Division of Economics and Sociology of the Reference Department of the New York Public Library and had studied and written on the needs of library education.[6] His survey of the library schools, therefore, was only a continuation of his interests in this area.

In the introduction to his report, Dr. Williamson stated:

> The primary purpose in preparing the following report was to present the existing conditions in this country with respect to training for library work in such a way that the educator and the layman interested in educational problems might be able to form a true conception of the steps that should be taken to improve this phase of the library situation.[7]

Dr. Williamson limited his survey to the fifteen "so-called professional schools" of the period, and he treated only incidentally training classes, summer schools, and other types of training agencies. He visited all the schools, studying their organization and methods during academic year 1920–21. He gathered information about curricula, faculties, entrance requirements, graduates, and financial status of the library schools by analyzing their reports. The collected information was then synthesized, interpreted, and presented in a report of nineteen chapters, the last of which contained a summary of findings and recommendations. Both the findings and recommendations were significant, but it was the latter that set new goals for the library schools and proposed a clear break with many of the traditional practices of library education.

Summary of Findings and Recommendations

Dr. Williamson believed that there were two general types of library work—professional and clerical—and that each type called for different kinds of general and vocational education. Through his survey of the library schools he found that the differences between the two types of library work had not been kept clearly in view in library organization and administration; consequently, they were "confused in the work of the library schools." His recommendations in the final chapter of his report were—among other things—that library schools confine themselves to training of the professional type, and that library-conducted training classes provide for the clerical type.[8]

Regarding the library school curriculum, he found "little agreement among the schools as to the relative importance of the different subjects." Cataloging, classification, book selection, and reference accounted for about half the students' time in library school, but even in these major subjects some schools gave "two to three times as many hours of instruction" as others. As a solution to these problems, he not only urged the formulation of minimum standards for the scope and content of the library school curriculum, but also stated that the content should be based on "frequent reanalyses of the training necessary for a professional librarian," rather than on tradition.

The entrance requirements of library schools were of very special concern to Dr. Williamson. He had worked hard to get the American Library Association to raise the standards in 1919. It was not surprising, therefore, that a fundamental conclusion of his survey was "that professional library training should be based on a college education or its full equivalent," and that anything less should "be looked upon merely as a step toward placing library schools on a strictly graduate basis." There was not a gap between any of his recommendations and actual practice that was wider than that seen here. Of the fifteen library schools included in his survey, only two required four years of college work for admission; the others required four years of high school work plus the passing of an entrance examination. However, the value and relevance of the examination to the real needs of librarianship were open to serious question. For Dr. Williamson found that the library schools, through these examinations, placed too much stress "on pure literature, history and the humanities in general," and too little stress on science and the social sciences. Furthermore, he found that the schools laid great emphasis on personality tests that he believed represented "an impressionistic method of very questionable value." He concluded, therefore, that the schools would "do well to abandon personality tests and admit on evidence of education and ability to maintain a high standard of scholarship."

The low level of education of library school teachers was also a topic of major concern. The meager training of a very large percentage of library school teachers justifiably raised serious doubts about their ability to teach on a professional and graduate

level. Dr. Williamson found that only 52 percent of the teachers
in library schools in 1921 were college graduates; that 42 percent
were teaching in the same school in which they were trained; that
93 percent had had no training in the art and science of teaching;
that 80 percent had had no experience in teaching before becoming a member of a library school faculty; and finally, that 32 percent did not have adequate experience in practical library work.
Consequently, he concluded that many library school teachers
were "not fitted to give instruction of high professional character
to college graduates." To strengthen library school faculties, he
recommended that salaries be increased in order to make teaching
more attractive to educated and "experienced librarians of the
highest ability."

Since he also found that existing library schools were operating
at only 60 percent of their capacity, Dr. Williamson did not share
the view that there was a need for several new library schools in
order to supply more trained librarians. Nor did he feel that the
shortage of librarians was primarily a recruiting problem, but
rather a problem of low esteem for librarianship. He came to
the conclusion that the shortage of librarians would be reduced
"only by making library service as attractive and desirable a
career for well-educated men and women as other learned professions."

Similarly, Dr. Williamson believed that librarians should receive
their professional training from institutions organized like the
professional schools of other learned professions. Library schools
conducted by public libraries served neither the best interest of
the library nor that of the profession and he felt that "the professional library school should be organized as a department of a
university, along with other professional schools, rather than in
public libraries, state or municipal."

Long before his survey of them, the library schools had been
criticized for not responding to the need for specialized library
training. Dr. Williamson found the allegation to be true, "partly
because of insufficient demand for specialized training and partly
because the schools . . . [had] been financially unable to expand
their work." Too few schools were providing specialized training
for children's, school, college, university, rural, and business libraries. He recommended, therefore, "that the first year of professional study continue to be general and basic, and that the work
of the second and following years be definitely and even minutely
specialized."

There seems to be a positive relation between continued professional study and improved professional performance. Dr. Williamson found, however, that the opportunities for continued professional education in library service had not advanced beyond summer schools, training classes, and institutes, and "most of these were designed only for the sub-professional grades of service." This led him to conclude that a new type of summer school and short intensive courses in library schools were needed, and to state "that some way should be found as soon as possible to offer instruction of the highest grade by correspondence method."

As a member, and later chairman, of the association's Committee on Certification and Standardization, Dr. Williamson was an early and strong supporter of certification. Since his survey revealed that "no generally recognized standards of fitness for library workers . . . [had] been formulated," he again recommended that the association create an agency to certify librarians and to promote all types of library training. He believed, moreover, that the library schools and other training agencies needed such a "representative and authoritative body to assist them not only in formulating standards, but particularly in enforcing standards agreed upon." He said that the Association of American Library Schools, because of "motives of self-interest and personal relationships," could not be expected to perform this function.

Three years before making his survey of the library schools, Dr. Williamson stated that "one of the most difficult and important problems of the whole range of library service is presented by the small public library."[9] His findings relevant to training of librarians to operate the small library did not lessen his pessimism about their future in 1921. On the contrary, the facts reenforced his judgment that well-educated librarians and leaders would "accomplish more in the long run for the small public library than the multiplication of library courses and training schools of the usual type." He further concluded that in order to use efficiently these properly educated librarians, it would be necessary to organize the isolated and independent libraries into a county unit system, thereby providing substantially larger administrative units.

In summary, Dr. Williamson's findings and recommendations covered eleven aspects of library service and library education: (1) types of library work and library education, (2) the library school curriculum, (3) entrance requirements, (4) teaching staffs and methods of instruction, (5) library school finances and salaries, (6) the library school and the university, (7) specialized study, (8) the need for more library schools and more students in training, (9) training in service, (10) certification of librarians and standardization of library schools, and (11) the problem of the small library. In each case, Dr. Williamson identified the key problems of the library schools, collected and interpreted facts relating to them, offered forthright criticisms of the programs of the library schools, and submitted specific recommendations for their improvement.

This study had been undertaken as a fact-finding survey for the sole benefit of trustees of the Carnegie Corporation. However, the subject of library education was of such widespread interest and importance that the corporation was advised to publish the report. Acting upon this advice, the corporation published the report in June, 1923, two years after the survey had been made.

Comments on the Report

If documented comments from library school directors and library administrators on Dr. Williamson's report may be used as indicators, the report did not strike the library schools and the profession "like a thunderbolt."[10] However, it did focus attention on the low quality of library education and isolated some of the important causes that produced it. It contained, moreover, recommendations for removal of the weaknesses of the existing library schools as well as for building them into true professional schools of a high order. Unfortunately, most of the library school faculties and directors who commented on the report failed to perceive its significance. Consequently, they missed the opportunity to improve the library schools from within through their own organization—the Association of American Library Schools.

The faculty of the New York State Library School wrote that Dr. Williamson's report was admirable and that it was the work of "an investigator of rare keenness and fair mind with the highest ideals for the promotion of library progress."[11] It agreed with him that professional and clerical training should be separated, "the curriculum enriched, entrance requirements standardized, the teaching staff strengthened, instruction improved, better textbooks prepared, and facilities provided for specialized and advanced study," and that some form of certification was needed. The faculty was not fully convinced "of the correctness of some minor findings and the wisdom of certain recommendations of the report." They questioned the validity of the statistical data collected from the various schools, and they believed the value of personality tests was not as questionable as Dr. Williamson stated. Finally, the faculty was concerned that Dr. Williamson had urged too strongly university affiliation for library schools without discussing the "great difficulty" that had hitherto prevented such an affiliation. But despite these reservations, the faculty believed Dr. Williamson had stated with precision some essential ideals of library education.

Josephine Rathbone, vice-director of Pratt Institute Library School, acknowledged the indebtedness of all library schools to Dr. Williamson for presenting in his report the financial difficulties that limited the development of the schools, but hastened to add: "yet being human, it is inevitable that we should find in his report some of that irritating quality that participators in the fray always feel in the criticism of those who are *sur le combat.*"[12]

This "being human" and "participating in the fray" apparently prevented Miss Rathbone from realizing that her attacks on the report were also attacks on the weaknesses of library education that had been expressed before, and not only by Dr. Williamson. Indeed, Carl Roden, chief librarian of the Chicago Public Library, stated that the report "contains little that is new, and even less that is startling, to one familiar with library affairs."[13]

Miss Rathbone, like the Library Workers Association four years earlier, objected to raising the entrance requirements to college level because there were persons in the profession who had been unable to attend college but who had "gained through reading and contact all that a college can give—culture, trained minds, broad outlooks." She pledged that Pratt would keep an open door for such persons.

Ernest J. Reece, principal of the Library School of the New York Public Library, appeared to have been optimistic as well as cautious about the significance of the report. He believed it would have a constructive effect on library education and library service only if all those interested and responsible could "be brought to join in the effort necessary to accomplish the desired changes. . . . The reformation," he said, "is a task for the profession at large—faculties, graduates, trustees, librarians and staff—and for those who control the sources of funds."[14] Since Mr. Reece did not submit any arguments for or against the report, it may be inferred from the above quotation that he probably agreed with most of Dr. Williamson's findings and recommendations.

June R. Donnelly, director of Simmons College School of Library Service, stated that "the chapter on field work was to her the most valuable and interesting in the Williamson report." Since "none of the theories expressed concerning the purpose of field work seemed to fit our purposes very well," she described what Simmons attempted to do through its fieldwork program.[15] It was one of the misfortunes of librarianship that Miss Donnelly did not direct her efforts towards making a judicious estimation of the recommendations that Dr. Williamson submitted for the improvement of all library schools, rather than towards trying to present a different image of Simmons by describing at length its fieldwork program.

The Library School of Drexel Institute was discontinued in 1914, and was not included in Dr. Williamson's report. However, one year before the report was published, Drexel was reopened and Anne W. Howland, its director, believed the report's publication marked "an epoch in the history of the development of library training only less important than the action of Mr. Dewey in organizing the first library school at Columbia in 1887."[16] She wondered, however, if library schools were "ready to accept the standards of other professional schools" and did not indicate whether she accepted or rejected the report's recommendations.

The director of Syracuse University Library School, Elizabeth G. Thorne, wrote that the findings of the report were not flattering but they were illuminating, and that the instinctive reaction of the library school would be "defensive." She advised, however, that a "close study of the report shows only the kindly knife of the surgeon wielding it in the interest of separating dead from living tissue."[17] While Miss Thorne did not agree with Dr. Williamson that more emphasis should be placed on the social and scientific subjects in the library school curriculum, and less on the humanities, she admitted this was a minor objection and considered the report not "as a criticism but as an encouragement to push on to better things" in library service and library education.

Tommie D. Barker, director of the Library School of the Carnegie Library of Atlanta, disagreed with the suggestion that professional and clerical work, as well as training for them, be separated—she did not believe this was either desirable or practical. On the other hand, Miss Barker came nearer than anyone else to perceiving a real need the report could have met. She noted that:

> Whether or not one sees eye to eye with the writer in his conclusions, none would underestimate the importance of the report in setting forth an ideal to be obtained and its value in bringing together so complete a body of facts relating to library schools. Apparently library schools are sailing an uncharted course. It is to be hoped that with this report as a starting point

the Temporary Library Training Board of A.L.A. will be able to work out such sailing directions as will enable library schools to attain a perfection of product as unquestioned as that which seems to be enjoyed by degree conferring institutions.[18]

Nina C. Brotherton, principal of the Carnegie Library School of Pittsburgh, felt "Dr. Williamson's long awaited report" could not "fail in its mission to provoke careful stock taking and self-examination on the part of all" who were responsible for the training of librarians.[19] However, she did not indicate whether the findings and recommendations would be accepted or rejected at Pittsburgh, or whether they contained the fundamental elements on which a new and better library-education system could be built. Dr. Williamson was calling for a reformation in library education, and reforms are much more the result of courageous and persistent action than they are the result of salutary pronouncements. Miss Brotherton apparently was not aware of this.

Alice S. Tyler, director of Western Reserve University Library School, was an eminent librarian and library educator when the report was published, but she could find nothing more worthy to say about it than to discuss the factors affecting the enrollment capacity of a library school.[20] Such an irrelevant response to the report by such an outstanding member of the library profession was undoubtedly a contributing factor to the less than cordial reception it received from the profession generally.

Miss Tyler's unimportant remarks, however, contributed no more to the formation of an indifferent professional attitude towards the report than the caustic reply of another prominent librarian, Arthur E. Bostwick, director of the St. Louis Public Library School. Mr. Bostwick's reply to the report was directed at an alleged misuse of figures relating to the seating capacity of the St. Louis school.[21] His acrid response was unworthy of a man of his stature and useless to those who were trying to build a better library system.

In contrast to Mr. Bostwick's attack, Phineas L. Windsor, director of the Library School of the University of Illinois, said:

The whole report is stimulating and cannot fail to affect the schools generally; we at Illinois are now going over our various courses in order to make changes and adjustments that have been suggested, in part, by the chapter on curriculum. Other chapters will be considered later and we hope that the report will be fully discussed at professional meetings during the year.[22]

Likewise, Marion Horton, principal of the Los Angeles Library School said:

> Dr. Williamson's visit to the school nearly three years ago stimulated us to an analysis of our curriculum, teaching devices, and finances. After reading his report we find that many of his suggestions have borne fruit in our present methods.[23]

Sydney B. Mitchell, associate librarian of the University of California, also believed the report would have a stimulating effect on the quality of education librarians received as well as the service they gave, and he concluded that:

> The failure of the American Library Association to accept and put into effect Dr. Williamson's early recommendations for national certification was a source of real sorrow to very many of us. We trust that such action will still come. We have done our best in California in the comparatively poor substitute of voluntary state certification but we based it as closely as we could on Dr. Williamson's recommendation so that if national certification comes we shall not be too far out of line.[24]

And, finally, as if in answer to his colleagues who questioned Dr. Williamson's qualifications to survey the library schools, William H. Henry, director of the Library School of the University of Washington, said:

> Dr. Williamson impressed me as a good academic scholar, one who had seen much of the inside of library service and not a product of any library school, and therefore clear of the prejudices for or against any one or all. His report shows a searching investigation of the institutions, and what seems to me a remarkable ability to place his finger upon both the centers of strength and of weakness of the schools as a group.
> I think I have read no report that showed surer aim at the vital point of the subject reported upon. I do not wish to imply that I can agree in all details with Dr. Williamson's conclusions, but I am frank to say his criticisms are the only vital ones that I have had the pleasure of reading. We have been so sentimentally good to ourselves that we have not dared to criticise ourselves searchingly.[25]

Also critical of the Williamson report were library administrators. However, their compliments and attacks were centered more on specific issues in the report. Consequently, they contributed more towards defining the essential problems of library education than the library educators.

Clarence E. Sherman, librarian of the Providence Public Library, not only agreed that there should be a division of professional and clerical duties, but also stated that the responsibility for making the division was more that of the libraries than of the library schools. He noted that the schools built their curricula "on the plan of preparing for definite service, for library work as it exists, not as it ought to be," and he believed they would continue to do so until the librarians in the field changed in their own libraries.[26]

On the other hand, Mr. Bostwick—commenting this time as a library administrator—rejected the recommendation that professional and clerical duties be separated. He argued that much of library work is so routine and intimately connected with the rest of the work "that no such division as that assumed in the report is possible, nor is it indeed desirable," and he was personally inclined not to accept it.[27] Similarly, Edwin H. Anderson, director of the New York Public Library, stated that Dr. Williamson's sharp line of demarcation between professional and clerical duties was "hardly justified under the conditions." Mr. Anderson believed that "a reasonable amount of this routine or drudgery is wholesome, in that it compels the professional man to keep his feet on the earth and not become enveloped in clouds of theory."[28]

The recommendation to affiliate all library schools with universities as graduate schools also had its supporters and nonsupporters among the library administrators. The supporters generally agreed with Dr. Williamson that such a move was the next logical step in the evolution of librarianship from a vocation to a profession. Those against affiliation were fearful that the subject matter of library service was too elementary to be put on a graduate level, and that such a move might be harmful to specialization. Dr. William W. Bishop, librarian of the University of Michigan, differed "from Dr. Williamson quite radically . . . on the proposal to make library schools graduate schools in the sense that they shall admit only students having a bachelor's degree. . . ."[29] Dr. Bishop believed this would be a mistake because certain important subjects in library science were too elementary to be studied with profit by graduate students. To insist that this be done would only render library school instruction more unsatisfactory and delay the development of library science courses with truly graduate content. Dr. Bishop further added that:

Graduate students should be put to graduate work under teachers trained to handle mature students. The elements should be gained in the undergraduate years, and they can be studied there without taking undue time from cultural and disciplinary courses. The analogy of pre-law and pre-medical training holds for pre-library training.

For Dr. Bishop, pre-library training during the undergraduate years was the next logical step in the evolution of library education and not its elevation to graduate level.

The director of the St. Louis Public Library, Mr. Bostwick, also objected to the affiliation of library schools with universities, but for a different reason than Dr. Bishop's. Mr. Bostwick feared that such affiliation would limit the opportunities to specialize in public library work. One may justly infer from his argument that he favored keeping some library schools in public libraries and also affiliating some with universities. "The advantage of having a certain number of schools conducted by libraries," he said, "is that they are enabled effectively to specialize in public library work, just as a school conducted by a university can, better than any other, train for the work of a university library."[30]

Mr. Bostwick's argument may have had some merit, but its obvious defect was that he wrongly equated the functions of a public library—a service institution—with those of a university—a research and educational institution. Apparently, he overlooked the fact that a university–connected library school could teach general concepts and principles that were applicable to all types of libraries, whereas a library school connected with a public library could hardly be expected to do so. It appears that faulty reasoning was used to justify the continuation of an existing and well–established condition in library education. Like so many other librarians of his time, Mr. Bostwick refused to accept changes in the status quo.

Dr. Williamson stated, at the beginning of chapter 19 of his report, that "at every point in our survey of the library schools and other training agencies, the need for higher standards, for standards of any kind . . . has been the outstanding conclusion." Perhaps because of this conclusion, library school directors—and only to a lesser extent library administrators—received his report with something less than enthusiasm. Most of them appeared to have ignored Dr. Williamson's stated purpose for making the study and substituted in its place the belief that the report was an attack upon the library schools. They apparently believed that it was their duty to defend the status quo in library education and to restore the image of the library schools that existed before it was tarnished by the report. Therefore, most of the leaders in library education not only failed to discuss the proposals recommended for the improvement of library education, but also did not seem to perceive the significance the report held for library education. An important opportunity was missed to create a solid movement for the improvement of library education. Instead, conditions were created for the beginning of a cleavage between the Association of American Library Schools and any agency supporting the findings and recommendations of the report.

The Report and the Board of Education for Librarianship

The Board of Education for Librarianship was established in June, 1924, almost a year after the publication of the Williamson report. While there may be some reason to doubt whether the report had any significant influence on the appointment of the Temporary Library Training Board, there can be little doubt that it greatly influenced the creation of the Board of Education for Librarianship.

The report was published in August, 1923; this was three months after the appointment of the Temporary Library Training Board and three months before it held its first open meeting on the problems of library education. Furthermore, the aforementioned comments from the library school directors and library administrators were published in November, 1923. All these persons were invited not only to the first open meeting on library education in January, 1924, but also to the second one in April; and, as already stated, twelve of the eighteen library schools in the Association of American Library Schools were represented. In May, 1924, the report was still the main topic of discussion.[31] But in addition to these factors, there were even more important reasons for concluding that the report influenced the creation of the Board of Education for Librarianship.

First, an agency was needed that would be responsible for coordinating all the activities pertaining to library education. This would include the distribution and control of all funds provided for the improvement of library education. The Association of American Library Schools had been virtually eliminated as such an agency not only because of its members' antagonistic reactions to the report, but also because Dr. Williamson and "the best library school authorities familiar with the situation and anxious to see standards raised" believed AALS was unfit for the task.[32]

Second, Malcolm G. Wyer, chairman of the Committee on Library Training, committed himself to the position that the report would have a significant impact on library education. He felt it would contribute greatly to a better library education system and he further concluded that the report had been "recognized as a searching and constructive analysis of library education, despite some dissension from, and criticisms of its conclusions and recommendations."[33] Mr. Wyer was also chairman of the committee when it recommended the appointment of the Temporary Library Training Board.

Third, and most important of all, Adam Strohm and the Carnegie Corporation welcomed the report because it aroused the library profession and supplied the layman with badly needed information about the state of library service and library education. In relating the role played by the report in helping the corporation to arrive at its decision to launch its ten-year program in library service, Robert M. Lester, secretary of the corporation, said it "presented existing conditions in such a way that the educator and the layman interested in educational problems were able to form a more accurate conception of the steps that should be taken to improve this phase of the library situation."[34]

This statement signifies that Dr. Williamson accomplished his main purpose for making the study, and that his report focused the corporation's attention on some of the critical problems of library education.

Adam Strohm was appointed chairman of the Temporary Library Training Board and he was also selected as the first chairman of the Board of Education for Librarianship. Like the Carnegie Corporation, he welcomed the report. Perhaps in response to Carl B. Roden, who felt that the report contained little new information, Mr. Strohm stated:

> Someone has said that Dr. Williamson tells us nothing that is new. Maybe not. Who does? But he has done *this*. He has vitalized the silent thoughts, the earnest hopes of a good many of us. We are aroused. I welcome this report.[35]

With this conviction about the significance of the report plus $10,000 from the Carnegie Corporation for the expenses of the Temporary Library Training Board, Mr. Strohm and the board proceeded to lay the foundation for the establishment of the Board of Education for Librarianship. It came into existence the next year, 1924, and the Carnegie Corporation gave it $26,000 to carry on its work.

Thus, despite the cool reception the library schools gave the report, the above factors leave little reason to doubt the positive influence it had on the creation of the Board of Education for Librarianship. The influence of the report and the work of the Temporary Library Training Board, however, did not end with the creation of the new board. Their "influences gradually led to a series of conferences to determine the manner and means by which the Corporation might be of assistance in improving library service and training."[36] As a result of the conferences plus additional research and planning, the corporation adopted, in 1926, the "Proposed Program in Library Service" that had been submitted to it in 1925. After its adoption, the program became known as the "Ten-Year Program in Library Service," in support of which the corporation voted "that sums aggregating four million, one hundred seventy thousand dollars ($4,170,000) be, and they hereby are, set aside to carry the program into effect. . . ."[37] The money was designated for three categories: (1) for support of existing schools, including Negro library schools—$1,440,000; (2) for establishment of a new type graduate library school—$1,385,000; and (3) for support of the American Library Association—$1,345,000.

It is impossible to known what the conditions of librarianship would have been like today if the Carnegie Corporation had not adopted its Ten-Year Program in Library Service. However, some idea of the program's impact on the development of library service and library education may be gained from an analysis of what it accomplished.

When the Carnegie Corporation adopted its Ten-Year Program in Library Service, there existed fourteen accredited library schools. Four of these—Atlanta, Los Angeles, New York Public, and St. Louis—were operated by public libraries. Drexel, Pratt, and Pittsburgh were operated by technical institutes, and the remaining seven schools were operated by colleges and universities. Of the fourteen schools, only Atlanta, New York Public, Pittsburgh, and Western Reserve had received support from the Carnegie Corporation before 1926. During the next ten years, however, the number of library schools that received grants increased greatly.

SUPPORT OF EXISTING LIBRARY SCHOOLS

Dr. Williamson, in his report, had strongly recommended that library schools be organized as departments of universities. It was becoming increasingly clear that public libraries were not suitable agencies for educating librarians and the movement to make library schools an integral part of universities was probably contemporaneous with the adoption of the Ten-Year Program in Library Service. Nonetheless, the Carnegie Corporation, more than any other agency or reason, quickened interest in the movement to locate library schools on university campuses and greatly facilitated such moves. The library schools of New York Public and New York State were the first to feel the influence of the corporation in this respect.

In 1925, the New York Public and New York State Library Schools were two of the best schools in existence. But even they were plagued by a lack of adequate financial support. This was especially true of the New York State Library School which had been founded in 1887 as the School of Library Economy of Columbia College, and which, two years later, was moved to the state library in Albany where its name was changed.

Despite its unequaled achievements in library education, the New York State Library School's existence, by 1925, was precarious. Its uncertain future was the result of a combination of factors: the impact of the Williamson report; the activities of the Temporary Library Training Board and the Board of Education for Librarianship; the attitude of the New York Regents Committee on the State Library and on Finance and Administration as well as that of the Commissioner of Education.

At a meeting held on April 13, 1925, in order to clarify the position and future of the Library School, the Commissioner of Education

> questioned the propriety of the state in continuing to maintain a library school, stressed the need of the space occupied by the school for the Department of Education, and noted that increasingly smaller numbers of graduates were entering library service in New York State.[38]

The Commissioner of Education failed in his attempt to close the Library School, mainly because the librarians attending the meeting prevailed upon the Regents to keep it open. Not only did the Regents vote that the state should continue its Library School, but it also stated that "every reasonable effort should be made by the Education Department to secure an adequate teaching staff at adequate salaries for the New York State Library School."[39]

However, within a year following the Regents' action, the trustees of Columbia University requested that the Library School be returned to its place of origin. With the unanimous consent of the Alumni Association of the New York State Library School, the Regents approved, on April 22, 1926, the return of the Library School to Columbia University.[40]

On March 3, 1926, Edwin H. Anderson, director of the New York Public Library, recommended to the board of trustees that authority be given to transfer the New York Public Library School to Columbia, contingent upon the proper arrangements. The recommendation was accepted and, on March 10, 1926, the trustees of the New York Public Library voted to transfer the school to Columbia.[41]

According to Mr. Reece, who was principal of the Library School at the time, Mr. Anderson became convinced the transfer was necessary because

> after the publication of Dr. Williamson's report "Training for Library Service" in 1923, and after appointment of the American Library Association Board of Education for Librarianship in 1924, the growth of new influences likely to affect all library schools was increasingly evident, but even more significantly as indicated by the experience of the Library School of the New York Public Library and by comparable practice in other professions, that connection with a university was essential if normal development was to continue.[42]

Because the Carnegie Corporation contributed annually to the support of the New York Public Library School, its financial needs in 1925 were not as acute as those of the New York State Library School. From 1911, when the New York Public Library was opened, to 1925, the corporation gave $255,000 to the school, which amounted to a major portion of the school's budget during the fifteen-year period.[43]

Despite the advantages of the school's becoming a part of a university, the trustees of the New York Public Library were greatly concerned over the possibility of losing the corporation's financial support for the school because of its transfer to Columbia. Hence, it was only after they had received the corporation's assurance that it would continue to support the school as a part of its Ten-Year Program that they approved the transfer.[44] Consequently, when the New York Public Library School and the New York State Library School were combined and gave birth to the School of Library Service which opened at Columbia University in September, 1926, the more than $250,000 given by the Carnegie Corporation played a vital role in the creation of the new university library school.

The Carnegie Corporation, through its Ten-Year Program in Library Service, helped to establish college and university centered library schools at the University of Denver, Hampton Institute, and the University of North Carolina, as well as assisting the Atlanta Library Training School to become part of Emory University.

Although the library school of the Los Angeles Public Library and the Riverside Library Service School were in existence at the time the Ten-Year Program was started, neither received any financial support from the program, nor did either become a part of an academic institution. The St. Louis Library, also in existence at the beginning of the program, received $18,850 from it, but never became a part of a college or university.

THE GRADUATE LIBRARY SCHOOL

The establishment of the Graduate Library School at the University of Chicago was the fulfillment of the aspirations and plans of many librarians as well as another significant achievement of the Carnegie Corporation's Ten-Year Program in Library Service. Many librarians, especially those at colleges and universities, had expressed the need for a library school that would offer advanced training in library science, but the conspicuous absence of the money necessary to establish such a school was always a formidable obstacle. This did not change until the Carnegie Corporation became a benefactor of library education.

As early as 1919, there had been a mounting concern among academic librarians about the lack of opportunities for advanced education in library science. In an effort to obtain factual information about the desirability of and opportunities for advanced library education, the New England Librarians' Committee on Graduate Training of College Library Assistants completed a survey on the question in 1919. In addition to finding that there was a need for better-educated librarians in the large academic libraries, the committee also found that there was a desire for a course leading to the doctor's degree in library science. On the other hand, there was very little demand for the doctoral degree in library science at that time.[45] Nonetheless, agitation for the establishment of a graduate library school must have continued: four years later, in 1923, a group of librarians in Washington, D.C., organized and presented a tentative prospectus for a National School of Library Science to be located in Washington. The Chicago Library Club was occupied during the same period on a proposal for the establishment of a graduate school in Chicago.[46] While it was formulating the minimum standards for library schools, the Board of Education for Librarianship conferred with both groups about their plans for a new graduate library school.

The board, at first, did not fully share the belief that there was a need for a new program. This may have been for two reasons. First, as the board grappled with the difficult task of organizing the existing library schools into a system of schools with higher standards, it undoubtedly could not see where another graduate school would fit into the scheme since there were already in existence "graduate library schools." Second, the Association of American Universities had advised the board against starting a doctoral program in library science, and suggested instead that librarians study for doctoral degrees in the established subject areas.[47]

The board, however, did not try to impose its views, nor those of the Association of American Universities, on the library profession—especially since the latter wanted such an institution. Instead, to obtain a consensus for or against the establishment of a new type of library school, the board held open meetings on the problem and discussed it with college and university administrators.[48] The combined effect of these activities apparently convinced the board that a new type of graduate library school was needed, not only for the improvement of library service, but also for the discovery and advancement of new knowledge in librarianship. In fact, the only means to make educators and laymen aware of the scholarly and professional nature of librarianship seemed to be such a school. Consequently, standards for an "Advance Graduate Library School" were included in the minimum standards of 1925, although no such school existed at the time. The advanced school, as conceived and planned, would differ from the existing graduate schools by being an integral part of a university which met the Association of American Universities' standards for graduate study. Its curriculum beyond the master's degree would "be limited to those students who by their previous study have demonstrated their ability to pursue a high type *either* of professional study *or* scientific research," and upon completion of the curriculum, a Ph.D. degree would be granted.[49] Thus, the board, after it was convinced of the need for a new type of graduate library school, planned for a graduate library school with standards of admission and programs of instruction and research that would be as rigorous as those of other professions and subject areas within universities.

Since the board had been convinced of the need for such a school, it was obviously not alone in its desire to see such a school established. The Chicago Library Club, which had already drawn up proposals for a new school, was vigorously seeking, in 1923, a benefactor for a graduate library school that would be located in Chicago. According to Mr. Lester:

On April 20, 1923, the Chicago Library Club submitted to the Carnegie Corporation a memorandum asking for a new-type library school, to be located in the city of Chicago. This school, they thought, should provide, in addition to other opportunities, facilities for which no satisfactory provision had hitherto been made—facilities for development of the cultural, literary, bibliographical, and sociological aspects of librarianship as a learned profession built upon ideals and charged with responsibilities as definite and as vital in their implications as those of any other learned profession, and requiring similar academic preparation to insure its highest development. Such a school, they said, should be an organic member of a university group, with the background, atmosphere, resources, and equipment afforded by such affiliation.[50]

This proposal—plus the Johnson report, the Williamson report, and work of the board—"came with cumulative effect to the attention of Frederick P. Keppel, who assumed his duties as president of the corporation on October 1, 1923."[51] After studying and analyzing the proposal and reports, Mr. Keppel stated: "The Corporation recognized that there was already in existence a number of library schools of excellent professional standing, but in their judgment there was no school which could be said to occupy for the librarian's profession a position analogous to that of the Harvard Law School or the Johns Hopkins Medical School."[52] Presumably, the corporation also recognized that many worthy projects never progress beyond the planning stage because of a lack of financial means to carry them out. Consequently, in order to guarantee the beginning and continued existence of this project, the corporation included in its Ten-Year Program of Library Service $1,385,000 for the establishment of "a library school of the highest professional type, which might be counted on doing for the library profession what the Johns Hopkins Medical School and the Harvard Law School have accomplished in their respective fields."[53]

Now that generous provisions had been made for the support of the advance graduate library school and standards adopted, agreement on its location was no small matter. Opinions were sharply divided on this question, and the final selection of the University of Chicago as the ideal university was more the work of Mr. Keppel than anyone else. The Executive Committee of the corporation approved Mr. Keppel's selection because: first, Chicago was

> the geographic center of the American library world; second, that the public and private libraries of Chicago offered extraordinary laboratory facilities; third, that the University of Chicago was an institution of the first rank and it was well balanced as to faculty and students, thus assuring a new and small school a good chance of becoming an integral part of the life of the University; fourth, and most important, the University had, in Dr. Burton, a President peculiarly well qualified to direct the organization of the new school since he had served many years as Director of the University Libraries.[54]

Whether Chicago was "the geographic center of the American library world" may have been a moot question, but there could have been little room for debate about Dr. Burton's interest in the establishment of a new type of library school. When the Chicago Library Club informed the Carnegie Corporation of the need for a new library school, Dr. Burton was one of the eleven librarians who signed the memorandum.* Unfortunately, Dr. Burton died before he completed the negotiations with Mr. Keppel with respect to locating the school at the University of Chicago. The work, however, was continued by his successor, Dr. Max Mason, who announced on February 26, 1926, that the University of Chicago would be happy to accept the endowment from the corporation in order to establish a library school. He also submitted, on April 20, 1926, a satisfactory program for the new school to the corporation. The Executive Committee accepted the program on May 4, 1926, thereby releasing the $1,385,000 for the founding of the Graduate Library School of the University of Chicago, and marking "an epoch in the history of education for librarianship."[55]

THE AMERICAN LIBRARY ASSOCIATION

The third and final element in the Ten-Year Program concerned the American Library Association, which had been the guiding

---

*The others were Sarah C. N. Bogle, William Teal, Alice Farquhar, Theodore Mueller, Sue W. Wuchter, Clement W. Andrews, I. C. M. Hanson, Theodore W. Koch, C. B. Roden, and George B. Utley.

genius of American librarianship. It is doubtful that a more elo-
quent testimony of the association's success in promoting the
idea of free library service for the benefit of all Americans can be
found than Mr. Keppel's conclusion that, "If one were to ask an
intelligent and well-informed foreigner as to the most important
contribution of the American people to human enlightenment,
the answer would in all probability be, the American Public
Library."[56] While Mr. Keppel could have obtained support for his
conclusion from numerous sources, it is certain that he relied
heavily on Dr. William S. Learned's study, *The American Public
Library and the Diffusion of Knowledge.*[57]

Dr. Learned was a member of the staff of the Carnegie Foundation for the Advancement of Teaching. For a time, however, he
also worked as a member of the staff of the Carnegie Corporation
and while there he gave particular consideration to library problems, especially the public library. Like Mr. Carnegie, he had an
abiding faith in the idea of self-education if the opportunities for
such were simply made available. Dr. Learned was also intrigued
by the potentialities of the adult education movement of the
twenties. It was, therefore, not unnatural for him to see in the
American public library a powerful arsenal for the diffusion of
knowledge. An astute observer of men and social forces, Dr.
Learned perceived that librarians and librarianship were at a
crossroads in 1923, not only in library education but also in
determining how the American Library Association could effectively exploit the social conditions of the time in order to provide
more and better free library service. His study is the fruit of his
research and thoughts on these problems.

Dr. Learned stated that the thesis of his study was "that a
modern public library organization can completely justify its
existence only by means of a diversified service that makes useful
ideas contained in print helpful and easily available to all of the
rational elements in the supporting population."[58] After identifying and analyzing the difficulties involved in the diffusion of
library service and knowledge, and further showing how they
were being successfully done on a limited scale, Dr. Learned concluded that the situation the public library faced in 1923 raised
"questions not as to its worth, but solely as to the direction and
character of its growth."[59]

The character and growth of the services of free public libraries
were more the responsibility of the American Library Association
than any other agency; and these were responsibilities which Dr.
Learned believed the association was peculiarly suited to carry

out, partly because it was not a large group, partly because it was inherently a homogeneous and unified group, but largely because the association was so situated and organized as to give from a common center library services of an impressive nature and on an extensive scale.[60] Money was the essential thing the association needed before it could realistically hope to carry out its responsibilities toward the small libraries, and this the Carnegie Corporation could give. Dr. Learned suggested, therefore, that the association's endowment be increased substantially.[61]

It is reasonable to assume, therefore, that the generous provision Mr. Keppel recommended to the trustees of the corporation for the support of the American Library Association was due no less to Dr. Learned's study than the high esteem he held for the American public library. Indeed, the third and final element in the Ten-Year Program in Library Service was $2 million for the American Library Association.

To summarize: The Carnegie Corporation gradually diverted its interests and resources from the prewar concentration on building libraries to the institutions that were training personnel to staff them. This redirection of interests and financial resources was greatly encouraged by the reports of Alvin S. Johnson, Charles S. Williamson, and William S. Learned, plus the results of several conferences on librarianship.

The proposal—based on these reports and conferences and submitted to the corporation by its president—was a commitment to give financial support to certain aspects of librarianship for a period of ten years. The corporation accepted the proposal and allocated more than $4 million to three main categories: (1) for the support of existing library schools, (2) for establishment of a new type of graduate library school, and (3) for support of the American Library Association.

The corporation also promoted Williamson's recommendation that existing library schools be organized as departments of universities. The Ten-Year Program's allocations, therefore, made it possible for many library schools to move into better facilities and in turn to raise the quality of library training to college and university level. More important than this, however, was the allocation of almost $1.5 million to found the Graduate Library School of the University of Chicago. This generous provision for the improvement of library education was unprecedented, and the opening of the Graduate Library School marked the beginning of a new and experimental era in library education.

Since the programs of all library schools were severely restricted by very inadequate financial support, the generous provisions made to them by the Carnegie Corporation through its Ten-Year Program in Library Service may be considered the most powerful force that affected the course of development of education for librarianship between 1919 and 1929.

5. The Association of American Library Schools

The Carnegie Corporation's Ten-Year Program in Library Service was the manifestation of a change of interest in the promotion of library service from that of helping to construct library buildings to that of helping to educate librarians. This change of interest established the beneficence of the Carnegie Corporation as the most important of several interacting forces that shaped the course of library education between 1919 and 1939. Another force was the Association of American Library Schools, although it was less conspicuous than the Carnegie Corporation.

This association was organized to solve problems relating to library education, as well as to establish and enforce certain standards that other schools were expected to meet and maintain in order to become members. Achieving membership in AALS was tantamount to becoming an accredited library school, a status recognized by the Committee on Library Training and the members of the profession at large. Following the examples of professional schools in other fields, the association determined entrance requirements, types of curricula, faculty qualifications, and administrative organization of all its members, and its actions received the approval of the field of librarianship. Hence, there was little question about the identity and esteem of the association between 1915 and 1924, the time between its origin and the establishment of the Board of Education for Librarianship.

The American Library Association, by giving its newly created board complete authority to establish standards for and to accredit all library training agencies, stripped AALS of the very activities that gave meaning and direction to its existence. Therefore, it is not unlikely that the association's anxieties about its role in the affairs of library education began with the creation of the board and were intensified by subsequent events.

After four years of less than cordial relations between the board and AALS, the latter finally appointed "a committee to consider and determine the relations of the Board of Education for Librarianship and the Association of American Library Schools."[1] This committee was appointed not only to clarify the position of the association relative to that of the board, but also as an attempt to regain for the association some of the influence it had exercised over all questions affecting library schools before the board was created. This last intention may be inferred from the findings of the committee which later reported that:

1. The Board of Education has not in general consisted of librarians who are experienced in library school teaching or administration; nor, with a few exceptions, has it consisted of librarians who are familiar at first hand with college and university administrative problems . . . .

2. While the Board has consulted with individual library schools, the recommendations of the Board when submitted for the approval of the Council of the A.L.A. have been submitted without formal consideration by the group of library schools as a body . . . . It might be well to suggest that all the Board recommendations, if they concern library schools, be submitted first to the A.A.L.S. for consideration, so that the Council will have both the recommendations of the Board and the judgment of the Association when the recommendations are acted upon.

3. The Board has laid a burden of reports and questionnaires upon library schools which should not be imposed upon them without their own collective consideration and approval.

4. Joint meetings of the Association and the Board have too often been merely meetings at which the representatives of the Schools were expected to do all or most of the talking. There has generally been no real cooperation evidenced in these meetings because the Board did not submit its own plans for consideration.

5. In the long run the profession will demand strong library schools, and strong schools are not likely to develop or to continue unless they can be reasonably independent in their determination of professional educational policies and in the conduct of experiments and research in the field of professional education. Such strength and independence are not likely to be encouraged if the Board continues to have as much power as it has. That power, of course, does not officially exist; but it is very real nevertheless.[2]

During the discussion of the committee's report, some members of AALS raised minor objections to the sweeping indictments against the board. They thought the composition of the board was satisfactory, and that if the association had not spoken out against certain policies of the board it was not because it was prevented from doing so, but rather because it had been too passive and poorly organized to make itself convincingly heard. However, there appeared to have been no disagreement among the members about the power of the board, its source having been concisely stated by one of the members: "It is the funds of the Board which give it its power over the schools. . . . It is an unequal combat between the Board and the schools."[3]

The identification of the sources of friction between the board and AALS should have been a step towards reconciling their differences. But such was not the case. The association was a closed organization and nonmembers could attend its meetings only by invitation; the minutes of the meeting at which the above grieviences against the board were discussed do not show that the board was represented. Since the board makes no reference in its official reports to these allegations, it may be assumed that no official efforts were made to reconcile the two groups. Moreover, whether or not there was a real basis for it, the association's fear of the board persisted to such an extent that its member schools were afraid not to comply with the many demands the board made on them. This point was emphasized by the Committee to Determine Relations Between the Board and the Association in its second report, in which it stated: "We all remember, too, that the Board approves and classifies Library Schools, and that approves [sic] carries great weight among librarians; and for this reason, few, if any schools will risk incurring the Board's displeasure by declining to comply with some of its requests. Partly for this reason, and no matter how great the 'burden,' most or all of the schools feel it necessary to comply in everything."[4]

The efforts of both the Committee on Relations between the Board of Education and the Association of American Library Schools and of the Activities Committee of the American Library Association failed to reconcile the differences between the two groups. After a trenchant letter from John C. Dana, librarian of the Newark Public Library, criticizing the activities of the American Library Association, especially those of the board, the association appointed the Activities Committee to study and report upon all the matters brought up by Mr. Dana.[5]

The Activities Committee found that because of the broad powers lodged in the board and its responsibilities covering all activities relating to library education, it received more criticism than any other agency of the association.[6] The criticisms, however, were more the result of the nature of the board's work than they were of the manner in which the board carried out its responsibilities. Concerning the relations between the board and AALS in particular, the Activities Committee said "anyone who has attended a meeting of the Association of American Library Schools cannot fail to be impressed by its evident antagonism towards the Board," and their relationship cannot be considered close.[7] Besides the excessive power of the board, the most frequent complaints of the library schools were: (1) the failure of the board to discuss proposals affecting the library schools with the association as a body; (2) a lack of knowledge about how the board decided which library schools were worthy of financial support; (3) dissatisfaction with the system of standardization and classification of library schools; and (4) dissatisfaction with the composition of the board. The Activities Committee acknowledged the right of the association to question whether a board composed of laymen was best qualified to examine and accredit the library schools. Since the existence of many library schools depended upon the actions of the board, this was a question that deserved careful scrutiny and continuous examination.

The findings of the committee led it to conclude that the system of classifying schools left much to be desired. In fact, it said that

> the work of the Board which presents the least satisfactory results is the attempt to classify the library schools. The classification adopted was inadequate in that it failed to provide a place for all existing schools. Two courses seem to the committee to be open; either to revise the classification as to provide a place for all schools or to discard the classification altogether.[8]

The charge relating to the excessive power of the board was probably the most difficult for the committee to deal with effectively. It noted that

> the Board was undoubtedly within its power to affect a school seriously if it should fail to accredit. This power is further strengthened by the fact that at the present time the Carnegie Corporation, largely if not wholly, is governed by the recommendations of the Board in making grants to various schools. This power may in natural circumstances be of great benefit to the profession in raising library training standards, but, on the other hand, if such power were used unwisely which to the best of our knowledge it has not been up to the present, it might cause a serious situation.[9]

Hence, it seemed that the Activities Committee had found itself in a dilemma. It agreed that the board had enormous power over the library schools and that such power was necessary in order to raise standards; it further agreed that the board had not abused its power. Yet it was likewise aware that this power, like all power, may be used to accomplish unworthy ends as well as good ones, if left unchecked as it was in this case. To the extent that the committee acknowledged this possibility, it tacitly agreed that AALS, though not yet abused by the board, was right to fear the board because of its unchecked power.

In order to resolve this dilemma and the other problems that were preventing harmonious relations between the board and AALS, the committee submitted the following recommendations: (1) that the air of secrecy both on the part of the board and upon the part of the association be reduced; (2) that the board issue a policy statement setting forth its procedure for recommending grants to library schools; (3) that library schools accredited by the board be placed upon the approved list without being classified; and (4) "that one member of the Board be nominated by the Executive Committee of the Association of American Library Schools, and another member be appointed by the President of the A.L.A. from members engaged in training outside of the accredited library schools."[10]

Although the Activities Committee's report and recommendations made some significant contributions towards better relations between the two groups, some essential differences remained to plague them. The chairman of the board, in response to the report and the recommendations, issued a statement that contained an explanation of the board's policy for awarding and recommending grants to library schools.[11] Whether or not the statement fully satisfied AALS, the document was highly praised by a group of outstanding librarians as one that should have removed any misapprehension about the board's purposes and activities, its actual and potential power notwithstanding.[12]

The board agreed with the Activities Committee that the system of classifying library schools, formulated to meet a situation as it existed, did not provide a place for all schools. However, it vigorously dissented from the view that the system should be discarded unless it provided a place for all schools. Standardization and classification could only be improved by constant revisions. And "in this important matter," the board stated, "the advice of the Association of American Library Schools has been sought. . . . At this moment a special committee of the Board awaits suggestions from A.A.L.S."[13]

But the board's extensive power and the inadequacy of the system of grouping library schools were not the only sources of friction between the board and AALS. There was also a serious dispute about whether the board's members were qualified to evaluate and accredit library schools, especially those connected with colleges and universities. The association expressed grave concern about the composition of the board when it stated:

> The Board of Education has not in general consisted of librarians who are experienced in library school teaching or administration; nor, with a few exceptions, has it consisted of librarians who are familiar at first hand with college and university administrative problems. The members as a body cannot be looked upon as experts in educational administration if that term is applied, as it generally is, to the distinctive policies and problems in administration confronting colleges, universities, and professional schools. Partly as a result, and with the best intentions on the part of the Board, some of the recommendations, standards and methods of the Board have not been so drawn up as to fit easily into the administrative practices or requirements of several of the library schools, especially those connected with colleges or universities.[14]

Three years later, the association had not changed its general attitude towards the board, which it considered made up of persons who were unqualified to rate questions regarding pedagogical and administrative aspects of library schools.[15] The Activities Committee doubtless recognized some validity in the association's criticisms because it tried to change the way board members were chosen to serve.

The committee accomplished even less towards reconciling the two groups through this recommendation than it did through any of the others because both rejected it outright. The association, while agreeing in principle that better representation of the educating agencies was needed, turned down the proposal with no other comment than "we look with disfavor upon the recommendation of the Activities Committee that one member of the Board of Education for Librarianship be appointed by A.A.L.S."[16]

Although the board was very concerned about defending both the competency of its members to perform their duties and the procedure which the Council had adopted for selecting board members, it, too, emphatically rejected the proposal to change the manner of selecting board members. The board reminded the critics who questioned the ability of its members to evaluate and accredit the training agencies that "of the eleven members of the Board since its inception, three have been directors of important library schools; another has been director for several years of summer schools; another, who has also been a director of a summer school, is the director of a new library school now organizing; another has been a professor of bibliography; and two have had intimate connections with training classes."[17] The board also recalled that its composition was discussed "when the Board was formed and the decision then reached has resulted in what has largely been a Board of lay members drawn by the Executive Board from the ranks of the A.L.A. at large. There is now, and has been at all times since the creation of the Board, strong representation of those who have had experience on the faculty of library schools." Consequently, the board refused to accept the Activities Committee's proposal to alter the manner in which its members were appointed because it would have limited the Executive Board's freedom to choose the best-qualified persons; because persons appointed according to the proposed plan would have been limited in their actions by their obligation to the group they represented; and finally because the board believed that under the operating system a wholesome representation of the varied library interests and activities was best secured.

Thus, the combined efforts of the Committee on the Relations between the Board of Education and the Association of American Library Schools and the Activities Committee amounted to little more than getting the board and the association to cooperate in the revision of the minimum standards for library schools. The

real sources of friction between the two groups remained un-
changed, and the association continued to exist in a precarious
atmosphere until 1936, when AALS faced some chilling and em-
barrassing facts which had not been so clear before. First, the
association accepted without challenge a statement from one of
its members that:

> certain activities that might well have claimed the attention of
> the Association have been successfully executed by the Board
> of Education for Librarianship, though there are those who
> hold the opinion that had the Association been alert to its re-
> sponsibilities ten years ago, it would have assumed certain
> phases of the work of the Board and in so doing would have
> gained prestige.[18]

Second, while claiming for librarians the same status and prestige that the Society for the Study of Engineering Education
claimed for engineering, the Association of American Law Schools
claimed for law, the Council of Medical Education claimed for
medicine, and the American Association of Dental Schools claimed
for dentistry, AALS was now painfully aware that it had not done,
and could not do, for library education and librarianship what
the above associations had done and were doing in their respective fields.

A third fact that emerged was that the association had been
incredibly passive, especially after the creation of the board, and
the influence of AALS on the development of library education
had been negligible. The association had been so inconsequential
in its own self-proclaimed field of activity that the greatest benefactor of library service and library education—the Carnegie
Corporation—had never even heard of it before 1936, and was
unwilling to give any money to help support it and its programs.[19]

After assessing the results of these facts about its past failures
and present weaknesses, the association embarked on a search
for some kind of activity or program, other than standardization
and accreditation of library training agencies, that would give it
a significant reason for existing. Curricula revisions, promotion
of research programs, and a proposal to unite with all other agencies concerned with professional library education in order to
form a division of professional training were all recommended.
All but the last were tried to the extent that extremely limited
time and money permitted, but by December, 1939, a meaningful
substitute still had not been found. The association was still grop-
ing for some important program that would restore the profes-

sional esteem it enjoyed before the board was created—an event which caused the association to lose the sole responsibility for creating and maintaining standards of excellence in the field of library education.

TRAINING SCHOOL LIBRARIANS

While the Board of Education for Librarianship and AALS were trying to accommodate themselves to each other and to adjust to the changes that were taking place in librarianship, the shortage of children, school, and special librarians was growing more acute, and continued to do so throughout the twenties and well into the thirties. Considering the complexity of the problem of constructing a library school curriculum suitable for the preparation of librarians for all types of library work, the long misunderstanding between the board and the association was indeed unfortunate. However, shortage of special librarians and the lack of suitable curricula to prepare them were apparently due less to the misunderstanding between the two groups than to other important factors: specialization in the first year library school curriculum versus a general first year library school curriculum, and the belief that a traditional liberal arts curriculum provided the best professional training for librarianship.

The specialization in librarianship that was clearly discernible in 1919 rapidly accelerated during the twenties and thirties, and the assessment of its impact on the personnel needs of libraries was a primary responsibility of the board. Hence, in 1925, the board began to focus attention on the need for more specially educated librarians, apparently assuming the library schools would modify their curricula in such a manner that librarians for all types of library work would be appropriately educated. Accordingly, the board pointed out that:

Libraries possessing collections devoted to special subjects are forced to fill positions from outside the library field because there are in most cases few and in some cases no librarians who have the knowledge of the subject essential to the work. This generally results in placing in charge a custodian who knows and appreciates the collection but does not know how to make it serve the users of the library.

There is a constant search for librarians for the smaller communities. . . . To secure librarians adapted to these communities is one of the problems to be solved. . . . The need must inevitably have its effect upon the library schools, in that . . . a great number of short courses must be offered to prepare local candidates for independent work.

There is an urgent need for librarians to take charge of the libraries in elementary, high, normal and consolidated schools. The problem is particularly pressing because legislation recently enacted in several states requires 'trained librarians' for school libraries.[20]

In addition to the shortage of special librarians, the board found a similar situation among children's librarians, adequately trained librarians to work in small public libraries, and school librarians. In its third annual report, the board stated:

> One of the chief concerns of the Board during the past three years of its existence has been the serious situation in regard to library work with children. Whatever the cause the fact is alarmingly evident that this fundamental part of the broad scheme of library service is menaced by the lack of personnel adequately equipped to carry it on successfully. Every year makes this more and more apparent.[21]

Finally, in 1929, the board called attention to still other areas of library service that were likely to be improperly developed because of a shortage of specially educated librarians and warned that:

> If people in the country are to be well served through county libraries, if adult education service of libraries is to be productively directed, if business and industry are to find librarians adequately trained for highly specialized service . . . education for librarianship must be expanded to include special curricula or special couses. . . .[22]

Thus, the board, during the twenties, gathered and reported some impressive information relating to the acute shortage of children, school, and specialized librarians. It also stated that these shortages hindered proper development of library service in all special areas of librarianship. The board suggested that the accredited library school should expand its curricula in such a manner that librarians for all types of library work could be prepared.

The accredited library schools' answers to the board's suggestion, as well as their relation to specialization in librarianship in 1929, were basically the same as they had been in 1919. The accredited library schools—all now members of AALS—were still committed to the principle that there was a core of library technique which, when mastered, would enable a librarian to practice in any type of library. The schools were only slightly less convinced that the first year of library education should be devoted to this core alone, and not to specialized training of librarians for all types of library work. Moreover, the library schools also believed that a four-year liberal education was the best preprofessional education for librarians and that time should not be taken during these undergraduate years for professional education.

Consequently, the association's position on the question of educating librarians for all types of library work became a divisive rather than a unifying force in library education. It succeeded in keeping the first-year curriculum mainly at the postgraduate level and more or less intact; it was no less successful in forging an alliance between school librarians and the teachers colleges, and in creating a curriculum dispute with the Special Libraries Association which lasted throughout the 1930s and beyond.

The dissatisfaction that resulted from a shortage of school librarians and which was mainly an expression of school librarians in 1919, had become a major concern of educators and school administrators by 1926. A survey of twenty representative city school systems showed that the superintendents felt the school library and librarian would play an increasingly important role in the school curriculum.[23] It was also found that there was not only grave concern about the shortage of librarians, but also about the kind of training they were receiving. This concern was expressed in the following manner by one superintendent:

> We have conducted a nation-wide search for librarians for our junior and senior high schools, and with great difficulty have brought together a group that seems fairly satisfactory, but we have been impressed at every turn by the great scarcity of good material in this field and by the lack of facilities for the preparation of librarians.[24]

This same school administrator, Jesse Newlon, of Denver, also expressed perhaps the prevailing opinion of many educators and administrators about what should constitute the training of school librarians:

> We believe that only college graduates should be employed as school librarians. . . . We believe that their professional prepa-

ration should include courses in education as well as adequate technical preparation for library work. In other words school librarians are teachers as well as librarians, and they should be familiar with the principle of education.[25]

Even more significant, in view of what later developed in the training of school librarians, the North Central Association of Colleges and Secondary Schools and the Library Committee of the Department of Secondary Education of the National Education Association completed their comprehensive report on the secondary school library and its needs as early as 1918.[26] In addition to quantitatively describing housing, equipment, book selection and use, financial support, and state supervision of the school library, these two groups stated that:

> The librarian in the high school should combine the good qualities of both the librarian and the teacher and must be able to think clearly and sympathetically in terms of the needs and interests of high-school students.
>
> The standard requirements for future appointments of librarians in high schools should be a college or university degree with major studies in literature, history, sociology, education, or other subjects appropriate to any special demands . . . upon the library. In addition the librarian should have at least one year of post-graduate library training in an approved library school and one year's successful library experience in work with young people in a library of standing.[27]

By "approved library school" the two groups meant those library schools which met "the standards of library training set up by the Committee on Library Training in the American Library Association and adopted by the Committee on High School Libraries in the National Education Association."[28] The American Library Association also endorsed these standards in 1920.[29] In 1925, a joint committee representing the National Education Association and the American Library Association completed the first set of standards for the elementary school library.[30] This committee also listed specific educational requirements for the elementary school librarian.[31] These requirements, like those set up for the high school librarian, called for radical changes in the curriculum of the accredited library schools if the latter were expected to train the elementary and high school librarians that were being demanded.

Thus, the school administrators as well as the aforementioned groups undoubtedly assumed that the school librarians specified in the standards for school libraries and called for by the changing school curricula would be trained by the accredited library schools. The board apparently assumed the same thing.

However, after presenting a series of factual and interpretative reports on the critical shortage of school librarians, and after seeing how ineffectually the accredited library schools were attacking the problem, the board concluded that inadequate facilities of the accredited library schools were not the only basic complicating factors preventing a solution, but also the library school's failure to provide the educators and administrators with school librarians who had had professional training in both librarianship and educational methods.[32] It further concluded that the library science courses that were being increasingly offered in the teachers colleges and normal schools were the result of an urgent demand for more school librarians, as well as a firm conviction held by educators and school administrators that this was the most practical—if not the most ideal—way to get the school librarians they needed. By approving the teachers colleges library education programs and by no longer supporting the old cherished notion that school librarians were best prepared in the traditional accredited library schools, the board helped to increase the supply of school librarians, but weakened its relations with AALS.[33]

The pedagogical revolution in the elementary and secondary schools raised the school library to a level of new significance, thereby creating a need for school librarians trained in the science of teaching as well as the science of librarianship. This revolution and the failure of the established library schools to modify their curricula in order to train the type of school librarians that were being demanded were not the only factors which produced the rapid increase in the number of library education programs in the teachers colleges; neither were they the sole factors that determined the scope and content of these new programs. The influence of "the great voluntary regional accrediting agencies" and the state certification laws were also important contributing forces.

It was predicted in 1919 that by 1923 at least eighteen states would have enacted certification laws for school librarians.[34] Although the state-certification-of-school-librarians movement did not spread as rapidly as had been predicted, fourteen states and the District of Columbia had adopted, by 1931, either voluntary or compulsory laws that regulated the employment qualifications of school librarians.[35] And by 1935 the District of Columbia and seventeen states required school librarians to hold certificates.[36]

Besides the state certification laws, the action of the regional accrediting agencies also helped to reduce the number of qualified school librarians, on the one hand, and on the other, to encourage the establishment of library education programs in teachers colleges. Apparently, it was clear that the accredited library school could not be depended upon to meet the demands, either in number or in content of education.

The North Central Association of Colleges and Secondary Schools, as stated above, was the first regional body to adopt a set of standards for secondary school libraries.[37] By 1931, all the other associations—the Middle States Association of Colleges and Secondary Schools, the New England Association of Colleges and Secondary Schools, the Northwest Association of Secondary and Higher Schools, and the Southern Association of Colleges and Secondary Schools—had set standards for school libraries.[38] The standards, however, were not uniform. The New England Association of Colleges and Secondary Schools and the Middle States Association of Colleges and Secondary Schools used general standards and included qualitative statements for the guidance of evaluating committees. The North Central Association of Colleges and Secondary Schools, the Northwest Association of Secondary and Higher Schools, and the Southern Association of Colleges and Secondary Schools used quantitative minimum requirements. It was this latter group, especially the Southern association, that greatly stimulated the establishment of library education programs in the teachers colleges, influencing both their scope and content.

Although membership in a regional association was voluntary, it was not taken lightly because these associations provided leadership in school improvement and stood for educational excellence in their respective regions. Schools, therefore, deliberately sought the assistance and prestige that membership in the association provided; and conversely, they tried to avoid the association's censure by meeting all the standards set by it.

The Southern association, probably one of the greatest stimulators of undergraduate library education programs in teachers colleges, adopted its first set of quantitative standards for school libraries in 1929. Concerning the qualifications of the school librarian, it specified that:

(1) Enrollment of 100 or less students, teacher-librarian with at least 6 semester hours in Library Science. Excuse from certain number of hours of teaching and thus allotted definite times for library work, with regular hours in the library. Sufficient student help trained by the teacher-librarian to keep the library open all day, but open only under supervision.

(2) Enrollment of 100 to 200 students, half-time librarian with a one-year course of 24–30 semester hours in an accredited library school, or half-time with college graduation, including 12 semester hours in Library Science.

(3) Enrollment of 200 to 500 students, full-time librarian with same qualifications and educational background as teachers, including 24–30 semester hours in an approved library school. One or two years teaching experience is very desirable.

(4) Enrollment of 500 to 1,000 students, same as above, with sufficient help and some experience in teaching or library especially desirable.

(5) Enrollment of 1,000 or more students, full-time librarian with college graduation and at least 24–30 semester hours in an approved library school. Teaching and library experience especially desirable, a good contact with children already established. For every 1,000 or major fraction thereof, enrollment, there shall be an additional full-time trained librarian.[39]

No one knew how many school librarians would be needed as a result of the Southern association's new standards. But a survey of 922 secondary schools in the association produced some facts which focused attention on the acuteness of the shortage. Of the 922 schools surveyed, only 54 met all the requirements for the school librarian; 344 were deficient in one or more points; 524, more than half, failed to meet any of the requirements for the school librarian.[40] Hence, the critical need for school librarians who were trained in both the science of librarianship and the science of teaching was clearly evident. Yet the accredited library schools, which had not already developed a curriculum for school librarians, made only minor changes in their curricula in order to satisfy the training need of school librarians. Consequently, AALS and most of its member schools missed an opportune time to work creatively and constructively with school administrators, educators, and the board to bring into existence a school library curriculum that would have been adequate for the twenties and the thirties. Even when a joint committee was formed to study the important question of educating teachers and librarians for library service in the school, AALS was not represented in its list of members.[41] The vital and complicated task of constructing a school library curriculum was therefore left to the teachers colleges by AALS and most of its member schools. The board gave encouragement and advice to the teachers colleges during the last half of the twenties, and it succeeded in accrediting some of the programs. But by 1932, the proliferation of library education programs in the teachers colleges was clearly beyond the board's control.

TRAINING FOR SPECIAL LIBRARIANSHIP

The Special Libraries Association, founded in 1909, likewise failed during the twenties and thirties to convince AALS that the first-year traditional curriculum did not provide adequate training for librarians going into special librarianship. As in the case of the school librarians, the prevailing position on the curriculum in 1936, as it was in 1926, was to acknowledge the existence of different types of libraries with their particular objectives and clientele, and on the other hand, to maintain that there was a core of library science that was equally common and essential to the education of all librarians, no matter what type of library staff they later joined.[42]

In order to change this prevailing opinion and to make known the training needs of its personnel as well as to explain its position on the subject, the Special Libraries Association established, in 1926, a Committee on Training for Special Librarians,[43] which later proclaimed that:

> The requirements for the special librarian are not the same as those made for the public librarian, university or school librarian. The business and professional world demand certain qualifications not needed in other kinds of library work. It behooves the Special Libraries Association to adopt general standards of requirements for preparation in the special library field.[44]

The Committee on Training subsequently formulated a set of "Minimum Standards for a Curriculum in Special Library Work to be Offered in Accredited Library Schools," and called for its acceptance on the grounds that it had been drawn up "in accordance with standards for other library courses as outlined by the American Library Association Board of Education for Librarianship."[45]

Apparently, the reaction of AALS to the proposed minimum standards was to ignore them, since no mention is made of them in its official proceedings. Nonetheless, outside the association, a lively debate ensued during the next twelve years, 1927–39, which resulted in a critical examination of the traditional library school curriculum in light of the training that was being requested by the Special Libraries Association. In pressing its claim for training of special librarians in the first-year curriculum of the library schools, the Committee on Training for Special Librarians concluded "that ideally a course for special librarians should be separate and distinct from the course given for general librarians. It should be especially planned for special librarians, and it should be elected by those persons who expect to pursue their profession in special libraries. The instruction necessarily needs to be adapted to the special librarian's work."[46]

The defenders of the first-year curriculum, which was designed to prepare librarians for general library work, replied that no library school or a dozen library schools could offer a specialized course for every kind of special library.[47] But assuming that they could, the library schools apparently still would have objected to the highly specialized curriculum. The need for such librarians was so limited that such narrowly trained persons had only limited possibilities for employment, and they had found that the general librarians had not only done notable work in all types of libraries but also that many were leaders in the Special Libraries Association.[48] Moreover, the defenders of the first-year curriculum agreed that the demands of the Committee on Training were impractical, at least in colleges and universities, since these did not readily offer curricula for the small number of students who were then going into special library work.[49]

In rebuttal, the critics of the first-year curriculum said the number of librarians who were going into special library work after graduation was small because the library schools were doing very little to prepare them for it. This conclusion was based on a very incomplete survey of 700 special librarians who were sent a questionnaire concerning their training and employment: of those replying only 8 percent said that they had been prepared for their work by the library schools.[50] The library schools, the critics charged, while claiming that specialization limited students' employment opportunities, produced no evidence to indicate that any individual who had specialized had, after graduation, encountered any difficulty in securing a desirable position.[51]

The above charges and countercharges were exchanged and examined by the critics and supporters of the first-year curriculum during the twenties and thirties. By 1939, attention was focused on four different solutions to the problem of specialization in library education and the training of special librarians. First, it was suggested that the first-year curriculum be kept general and that a second-year program devoted to specialization be added. This was the oldest approach to the problem and it had been tried long before 1919 by the two-year library schools. It was not until after the Williamson report, however, that it achieved widespread attention. But its application as a solution fell short of expectations because the courses that were offered were not basically different from those the students had taken in the first-year curriculum. Moreover, the second-year curriculum was an inadequate solution because only a few students could afford to spend a second year in library school.

A suggestion that the first-year curriculum be divided into two parts was offered as a second solution. According to this proposal, the core of the first-year's work would be telescoped into the first half of the year, the second half being for specialization. The essence of this proposal was first presented by June R. Donnelly in 1921. However, it was not widely adopted between 1921 and 1939, probably because of the reason its originator predicted that it would not be—a lack of funds to finance it.[52]

A third possible solution came from a critic of the first-year curriculum who suggested that perhaps special librarians were trying to solve their training needs the wrong way by attempting to develop a program as a variation of the first-year curriculum. He then stated:

> It is far from impossible that more efficacious results would be obtained from urging the introduction of courses in library training into the graduate schools dealing with engineering, social science, economics, and the like. This training for special librarianship would develop . . . as an addition of an abbreviated library school program to other graduate work.[53]

This was the most radical of the solutions suggested, and this may account for the fact that it was not taken seriously.

The fourth and final proposal grew out of the debate on specialized training that was carried on during the 1920s and 1930s, and was formally offered by Harriett Howe in 1938.[54] Miss Howe suggested that, since there were more likenesses in all types of libraries than differences, a curriculum be developed that would not only give the student a thorough training in the likenesses, but would also deal with the differences and the student's special interests through seminars, special projects, and term papers. This type of curriculum, she further suggested, could be supplemented by intensive field work in the type of library that was of interest to the student.

Miss Howe's suggestion carried the advantage of having been experimented with at the Denver School of Librarianship, and it was found to be both practical and satisfactory.[55] Moreover, it was a curriculum of this nature that the special librarians said they would accept if they could not obtain their ideal program.

Thus, the debate about special library training was carried on outside of AALS during the twenties and thirties. The proposed solutions to the problems were significant and they moved library educators one step further towards realizing the need to prepare librarians for all types of library work. It is important to note, however, that no apparent mention was made of the proposals submitted by Ernest J. Reece in 1923.[56] Because of the potentialities that his proposal embodied for reconstructing a significant library school curriculum, it was perhaps unfortunate that they were omitted from consideration.

Among other things, Mr. Reece suggested that the firmly entrenched belief that a bachelor's degree was the essential prerequisite to the study of library science be subjected to a fresh and critical examination. Such an examination, he believed, would reveal the wisdom of liberalizing this prerequisite and of introducing some library science courses in the undergraduate curriculum. Mr. Reece further suggested:

> Persons therefore who aimed to qualify for professional status could do so by four years of undergraduate work, one of which was of a professional nature. Those who wished could go on, and by no more expenditure of time than is now necessary for one who seeks a bachelor's degree and elementary professional study, secure a master's degree, and not only fit themselves for higher grades of the service, but assure themselves the academic recognition which present library degrees cannot command.[57]

Mr. Reece, paradoxically, submitted his proposal at an opportune time: in 1924, when there was an intensive search for new directions in library education. Yet it was passed over, despite the enormous potentialities it possessed for building an undergraduate base for library education as well as for preparing students to begin specialization at the first-year graduate level. If his proposal had been tried, it is quite probable that librarians for all types of library work could have been prepared during their first year of graduate study and the debate of the twenties and thirties may not have taken the turn it did. Mr. Reece's proposal was not accepted and the stimulating discussion which did take place was carried on outside of AALS; but it apparently affected the thinking of the group anyway because in 1938 the association created a Committee on Curriculum Revision.[58] The next year the chairman of this committee strongly criticized special librarians for being so confused about the type of training they wanted the library schools to provide and for their lack of factual information on library education, and challenged them to give the library schools valid criticisms and concrete proposals.[59]

Certain conclusions seem appropriate here. Partly because of the prolonged antagonism between it and the board and partly because of its defense of the traditional concepts and patterns of library education, AALS had a negative effect on the development of education for librarianship between 1924–39. Before the board was created, AALS established standards of training and accredited library schools. These activities constituted its most meaningful and significant work. It therefore lost considerable professional esteem when the American Library Association transferred standardization of library training and accreditation of library schools to the board, and for several years it encountered difficulties in adjusting to the responsibility and authority of the board.

The Association of American Library Schools committed itself to a defense of the traditional concepts and patterns of library education, but the board was responsible for modifying existing library education programs and concepts in order to provide suitably trained personnel for all types of libraries. This fundamental difference in objectives was another source of irritation that prevented the two groups from working creatively to solve the complex and important problems of training school and special librarians.

The shortage of school librarians was greatly increased by the pedagogical revolution in the schools and by the requirements of regional accrediting associations. The association's failure to respond to this acute shortage by modifying the first-year curriculum in library schools to provide the training needed by school librarians contributed to the board's decision to encourage teachers colleges to offer library education programs for school librarians.

Similarly, this failure to modify the traditional curriculum greatly stimulated the discussions about the library training that was needed by special librarians and their inability to obtain it in the accredited library schools. These discussions were carried on mainly outside of the association and without its participation, but they undoubtedly aroused some concern within the group because it subsequently appointed a curriculum-revision committee. By 1939, there was evidence that the board and the association were willing to work together for the improvement of library education and indications that the latter was giving serious consideration to a revision of the traditional first-year library school curriculum in order to provide training for librarians of all types of libraries. But the association's loss of self-esteem and its apprehensiveness about the plans and actions of the board—plus its conservative attitude about the values of the traditional first-year curriculum—resulted in an unfortunate waste of talent and time, thereby delaying the establishment of a vigorous partnership between itself and the Board of Education for Librarianship.

6. Education for Librarianship, 1939: Problems and Conclusions

The Great Depression did more than force the Board of Education for Librarianship to curtail its expansion program in library education. It also provided a decade to evaluate the work of the board, to identify problems, and to see the emerging forces that were destined to play an increasingly important role in shaping the course of development of library education.

When the board was created, it was committed to many broad responsibilities and was delegated commensurate powers for dealing with them. While carrying out its duties and exercising its powers, the board often encountered criticism and opposition from librarians as well as from library school administrators and teachers. Some of the criticism was rigorous and unjustified; some justified and constructive.

THE MINIMUM STANDARDS AND ACCREDITATION

The board's minimum standards for library training agencies and its accrediting activities aroused grave concern and attracted severe criticisms.[1] This was probably inevitable because of the complexity of constructing and applying standards to educational agencies already in existence. By constructing a set of standards that accommodated nearly all the library schools existing in 1925, the board had attracted the very criticism it was trying to avoid, and the few schools omitted from these standards proved fertile ground for the seed of discontent.[2] But even more important, there is doubt that the minimum standards raised the level of library education.

The minimum standards for library schools, as stated previously, were quantitative and were divided into four categories: junior undergraduate, senior undergraduate, graduate, and advanced graduate library schools. No significant curriculum changes were required of the library schools after being assigned to their respective categories since the categories were determined by the results of a study of these same schools. Hence, the category of accreditation each school received simply put an official stamp of approval on its existing methods and permitted it to continue in much the same manner as before, restricted now only by the limitations of the group into which it was classified. The limitations, however, were also without meaning since they did not prevent library school graduates of a junior library school from competing with graduates of the graduate library schools for the same professional positions.

Another charge made against the board's minimum standards for library schools was that because they were quantitative, very little freedom was allowed for local initiative and experimentation. Consequently, there was the constant danger and complaint that they would bring about over-standardization of library education. Soon after the standards were adopted in 1926, a special committee appointed to investigate the standardizing effects of accrediting agencies concluded that "probably no other phase of education for standardization presents more thoroughgoing machinery for standardization on a nation-wide basis than does library training under the plan now going into operation under this Board of the American Library Association."[3] The charge was premature and exaggerated since the board never attempted to obtain the degree of standardization explicit in the minimum standards. Insomuch as many schools felt that their freedom to experiment was being unreasonably limited, the fear was real, and this became a major complaint of AALS. (It is interesting to note that the Graduate Library School of the University of Chicago, which was experimenting with a new library school curriculum, did not seek accreditation until after the minimum standards had been revised to a qualitative basis.)

The board, however, was able to perform its accrediting activities under the quantitative standards until 1933. There were many who believed that the widely different library education programs of 1924 compelled the use of some such quantitative standards and that the board had very likely done the best it could with a complex situation. The subcommittee appointed to study the work of the board undoubtedly summarized the feeling of many librarians when it stated:

> Perhaps no single part of the work of the Board of Education has aroused so much feeling as its classification of library schools. Members of the Board are keen to point out that this work was not sought by them but was placed upon them by the American Library Association in creating the Board of Education for Librarianship. The task has not been a welcome one or an easy one, and it has been performed, we think, with judgment and good sense. The wisdom of attempting such a classification may well be questioned, and there is no doubt that a certain amount of opposition to the work of the Board of Education has arisen from its actions in carrying out the mandate of the Association which required it to classify library schools as well as to accredit them.[4]

The board was aware that the minimum standards had limitations and did not deny some of the charges made against it.[5] However, it denied the charge that it was trying to make all library schools uniform and that its application of the standards restricted the freedom of the library schools; it also rejected a proposal that the standards be discarded unless they provided a place for all library schools. It agreed instead with apologists and critics who proposed a revision of the standards.[6]

The Association of American Library Schools did not participate as an official body in the formation of the minimum standards in 1923–25. This was a grave mistake for both the association and the board. Its consequences aggravated the misunderstanding that existed between AALS and the board, preventing them from working together for the improvement of library education. Before beginning its revision of the standards, the board demonstrated that it had benefited from the mistake by inviting AALS to appoint a committee to help with the revision; the invitation was accepted and the committee appointed.[7]

Thus, because of the limitations of the quantitative minimum standards for library schools and the constructive criticism they engendered, the board and AALS began a complete revision of the standards in 1930. Besides the changing trends in library service and their own objectives, both bodies were governed in their revision by the objectives of the North Central Association in replacing the quantitative standards with qualitative ones for institutions of higher education.[8]

Three years later, in 1933, a new set of standards for library schools was completed and approved.[9] The standards were, of course, not perfect, but they were a substantial improvement over those adopted in 1926. Even more important, they were qualitative and represented the results of a broad spectrum of criticism, knowledge, and experience.[10] The new minimum requirements stipulated "what, rather than how much, should go into a curriculum" and no attempt was made "to state by credit hours, by class hours, or by any quantitative statement what should constitute a "library school curriculum."[11]

The key provision of the new minimum requirements was probably the one for classifying library schools, which was explained as follows:

> The classification of library schools neither includes nor implies a comparative rating or grading of the schools. Provision is made for three classes of library schools, Type I, Type II, and Type III.
>
> Type I comprises library schools which require at least a bachelor's degree for admission to the first full academic year of library science, and/or which give advance professional training beyond the first year.
>
> Type II consists of library schools which give only the first full academic year of library science, requiring four years of appropriate college work for admission.
>
> Type III consists of library schools which give only the first full academic year of library science, not requiring four years of college work for admission.[12]

The adoption of the new minimum standards with the above key provisions effectively stopped the widespread criticism of the board's accrediting activities. But there were other aspects of the board's work that attracted the attention of the critics and supporters.

TRAINING SCHOOL AND SPECIAL LIBRARIANS

In 1919, the question on how to train school and special librarians was asked and was not answered. The pedagogical revolution in schools and the influence of regional accrediting associations between 1919 and 1939 made the school library a curriculum enrichment center, supervised by a professionally trained librarian. Similarly, the recognition of research as the lifeblood of competi-

tive business created positions in special libraries requiring librarians who were capable of acquiring and organizing up-to-date
information on business, commerce, and industry. The traditional
one-year library school curriculum, however, was unsuited for
training the types of school and special librarians that were
needed in increasing numbers. This was because the curriculum
was based on and governed by the following assumptions: (1)
there was a core of library knowledge that was common to all
types of libraries; (2) that this core should constitute the one-year
library school curriculum; (3) that all librarians should master
it before being allowed to specialize in any type of library work;
(4) that the accredited library schools should offer only this body
of knowledge during the first year of library training; and (5)
that the library schools should not change the first-year curriculum in order to train school and special librarians.

By adhering to the unified one-year curriculum which trained
only general librarians, AALS—which included all the accredited
library schools after 1927—frustrated the board's limited efforts
to increase the opportunities for training school and special librarians. Consequently, the board increased the number of school
librarians by encouraging teachers colleges to offer library education programs for school librarians. But in so doing, it also encouraged the growth of a group of library training agencies over
which it held even less control than that which it held over the
accredited library schools. The number of teachers colleges that
offered training for school librarians increased rapidly and their
programs were of uneven quality. This increase, however, was due
more to the regional accrediting associations' standards for high
school librarians than to the encouragement given by the board.
Nonetheless, AALS strongly criticized the board for its role in the
growth of the library education programs offered by teachers
colleges.

The difficulty of providing a library education program for
school librarians was further complicated by the certification laws
being enacted in many states. The power inherent in these laws
reduced the board's control over the programs that were offered
by the teachers colleges. These programs were established to prepare school librarians to meet the certification requirements established by the states and regional accrediting agencies. The
board's standards, therefore, had little influence on the quality
of school library training unless they coincided with those certification requirements. Similarly, the accredited library schools' curricula for school librarians were sometimes rendered ineffective

by states' requirements for certification of school librarians. Frequently, these complicated requirements permitted denial of certification to the graduate of an accredited library school's program for school librarians because the person had not taken the number of required hours in certain subject areas that were specified for that category of certification. Yet this same librarian could and often did turn to children's library work in a public library. These were the complex conditions existing in the area of school library training in 1919, and there was no agency yet in existence which possessed the necessary power to reconcile the divergent programs.

Although recognized in 1919, and discussed repeatedly during the twenties and thirties, the problem of education for special librarians remained unsolved in 1939. The duties of special librarians continued to grow in scope and importance, but the traditional pattern of the library school curriculum persisted. No modifications of the first-year library school curriculum were made because of the basic assumptions stated earlier, and also because of the wide divergence of opinion concerning the methods of training special librarians. The discussions focused attention on these different opinions as well as a number of proposals to reconcile them. But here too the absence of a strong unifying agency was decisive. Unfortunately, the discussions on the training needs of special librarians took place largely outside of AALS. Hence, their influence on the accredited library schools was not as creative and constructive as it might have been had there been a free exchange of opinions and proposals between special librarians and the schools. Once again, there was no agency with sufficient power to establish such an exchange. The board, although still the official agency on all questions of library education, did not assume this vital responsibility.

ADVANCED GRADUATE STUDY AND THE Ph.D. IN LIBRARY SCIENCE

Advanced graduate study and the Ph.D. curriculum in library science, which was first offered by the Graduate Library School of the University of Chicago, aroused considerable concern among librarians and nonlibrarians alike, and was subjected to rigorous criticism between 1930 and 1939. There was serious doubt that advanced study in library science was necessary; indeed there were those who seriously questioned whether or not formal study of library science was essential to becoming a successful librarian. Thus, the Ph.D. curriculum was only cautiously accepted by some, while others strongly advised against it.

Understandably, the pressure for graduate study in library science was generated mainly by college and university librarians, whose efforts aided in the creation of the Graduate Library School. While stating that graduate study in library science was needed and that it should be comparable in quality to that offered by other graduate schools, the supporters of graduate study said very little about the nature of the curriculum and the degree that should be awarded for its completion. Yet, by 1924, the trend of thought on these questions was becoming quite clear. Although two members of AALS were offering a second-year program in library science in 1924, no library school was planning or was prepared to offer a Ph.D. curriculum. The association's committee on library degrees gave no consideration to the question of a Ph.D. degree in its deliberations.[13] Hence, provisions for this degree seem to have been of no official concern to the association in 1924.

But the Board of Education for Librarianship was very much concerned with this question, since it wanted to include a proposal for an advanced graduate library school in its minimum standards. Therefore, it sought the advice of the Association of American Universities, which subsequently advised the board against offering a Ph.D. in library science.[14] The association suggested instead that librarians take the Ph.D. in one of the established subject areas. Contrary to this advice, the board included a proposal for a Ph.D. curriculum in the 1926 Minimum Standards for Library Schools.

Since the Graduate Library School was expected to raise the level of professional training for librarianship as well as its prestige—as other graduate schools had done for other professions—and since it was established and governed by the same principles that regulated other graduate schools of the University of Chicago, the Graduate Library School offered a Ph.D. curriculum in library science as a logical development within the university. Further approbation was given its action by the Association of American Universities when, clarifying earlier advice given to the board, it stated that each institution had the authority to determine the degree to be granted upon completion of its curriculum.[15]

Five years after the opening of the Graduate Library School, a group of eminent librarians convened to study trends in education for librarianship, and particular consideration was given to the Ph.D. in librarianship. These librarians raised a basic question concerning its relative value and concurred with the Association of American Universities' first statement that advanced study in a subject area would be more profitable. The substance of their conclusion was explained in the following extract:

> The Committee discussed at some length the problem of the candidate for higher degrees, especially the doctorate. Since the library embraces the universe of knowledge, and since the methods and techniques of library practice are fairly simple, it seems wise for the candidate for the doctor's degree to devote himself to a broadening of his powers along avenues which he may tread in his professional service of the public. For example, important though cataloging may be, it would not seem profitable to take a doctor's degree in that special subject; and the same statement holds true in regard to most subjects in the library school curriculum.[16]

The judgment of these librarians did not deter the Graduate Library School as it continued to develop its Ph.D. curriculum, nor did it lessen the criticism of the program. In 1936, Walter A. Jessup, an officer of the Carnegie Corporation, charged, in a memorandum to the Carnegie Corporation, that the leadership in the field of library education was "committed to the importance of training librarians in such a way as to make them academically respectable by conformity to the institutional requirements for the master's and doctor's degrees."[17]

Finally, Ralph Munn, librarian of the Pittsburgh Public Library, in his special report to the Carnegie Corporation, also expressed reservations concerning the value of a Ph.D. degree in librarianship. He observed "that the directors of leading library schools are themselves not agreed as to whether the doctorate should be taken in library or a traditional subject field, and the content of even the second year is in dispute." Consequently, he recommended that:

> Since the pursuit of the doctorate in librarianship is so open to question, schools which limit their curricula to a second year should not now be encouraged to add further years leading to the Ph.D. degree. Such experiments as are being carried out at the University of Chicago are sufficient for a later appraisal of their worth.[18]

No new Ph.D. programs in library science were started before 1939. But this was probably due more to a lack of funds, capable teachers, and adequate facilities than to the impact of Munn's recommendation.

But serious concern about the advisability of offering a Ph.D. curriculum in library science was not the only question that pro· voked criticism of the Graduate Library School's curriculum; there was also a strong feeling that continued enrichment of the book-centered first-year library school curriculum was being en· dangered by the great emphasis placed on the second-year cur· riculum for which a master's degree was granted. There was a deep and widespread belief that the most important knowledge a librarian could have was knowledge about books: not only knowl- edge about their history, but a wide acquaintance with their contents and bibliographies. The adherents to this belief were convinced that knowledge about books should be the essence of a librarian's training. They therefore criticized the trend of gradu- ate study in library science because they believed there was too much emphasis on techniques, especially those of research. They argued that librarianship's

> fundamental and dominating purpose must be educational; its primary purpose is educational, the most important qualifica- tion for a librarian must be education. More specifically . . . our purpose is what Mr. Jewett described in 1853 as a 'diffusion of a knowledge of good books, and enlarging the means of public access to them.' Does it not follow, then, that the most important qualification for librarianship, the qualification that underlies all others, is 'a knowledge of good books,' with the high standards of education which that presupposes?[19]

This belief in the supreme importance of book knowledge to the librarian was also shared by William S. Learned, a strong supporter of library education and a member of the Carnegie Foundation. He also believed that too much emphasis was on advanced graduate study and that that was not the librarian's essential need. Learned said:

> The outstanding need in library education is the identification, selection, and stimulation of a type of mind that knows books comprehensively in a given field, or in given fields, and is able effectively to recognize and minister to the needs of individual groups in the use of these books. Library technique is a neces- sary but minor part of this equipment.[20]

Munn shared this view, and in his report to the Carnegie Cor· poration he focused attention on the harm that could be done to the book-centered first-year curriculum by over-emphasizing re- search and advanced study in library science. He reminded library educators that "successful librarianship is to a great extent dependent upon (a) general education with special emphasis upon a wide knowledge of books, (b) common sense and other personal traits, and (c) a relatively small amount of special library technique."[21] Munn further stated that the primary objective of his report was in calling attention to the fact that most of the current discussion was so exclusively limited to advanced library education that there was grave danger of failing to improve the one-year curriculum in order to establish the much-discussed advanced program in library education. He summarized this position in the following manner:

> This report, while fully recognizing the importance of advanced studies in library schools, is intended to serve somewhat as a corrective to the present tendency toward almost complete absorption in a protest against the growing affection which many librarians are showing for the pseudo-scientific methods and jargon which they are borrowing from the schools of education.
>
> The success of our library program as a whole still depends largely upon the supply of an intelligent, well educated, socially minded body of librarians to staff the average type of public and college libraries. . . . Prevailing and probable salary scales do not warrant more than one year of library school training for the rank and file of librarians, nor does the nature of their work demand it. Let us not lose sight, then, of the basic one-year courses, but strengthen them wherever possible.[22]

These objections to emphasizing the importance of graduate study and the Ph.D. degree in library science by sacrificing the enrichment of the book-centered one-year curriculum raised another fundamental question: was formal study in a library school essential to becoming a successful librarian? Neither librarians nor library educators would give an affirmative answer to this question, mainly because there were among them several distinguished librarians who had never attended a library school. It was such a group of prominent librarians and library educators who assembled to discuss this question and found, on the one hand, that most of the recent appointments to high positions were library school graduates, but stated, on the other hand, that:

> We believe that specialized scholarship with or without library school training is always likely to form a basis for appointment to higher positions in the library profession. We are confident

that the doors should not be closed to persons offering this kind of training. To cite but a few instances: the Librarian of Congress, the librarians of the Boston, St. Louis, and Chicago Public Libraries, of the University Libraries of Yale, Harvard, Princeton, Michigan, Chicago, and North Carolina, are not library school graduates. It cannot be argued that these persons have not done their part toward carrying on library work successfully and raising its standards. On the other hand, the librarians of the New York, Brooklyn, Baltimore, Pittsburgh, and Cincinnati Public Libraries, and of the Universities of Pennsylvania, Illinois, California, and Minnesota, are graduates of library schools. It will be seen, therefore, that while there is a definite tendency toward depending on library schools for the more important positions in library work, graduation from a library school is not yet a *sine qua non* for advancement in librarianship.[23]

This conclusion was undoubtedly disquieting and probably increased the difficulties for those who were trying to understand the nature of librarianship, and who were also trying to establish the study of it as an academic discipline in colleges and universities.

The above criticisms may have had some negative effect on the Graduate Library School at the University of Chicago, but its purpose was not changed nor was it prevented from guiding the course of education for librarianship into new directions. Before 1928, no organized attempts were made to create a body of systematic knowledge about librarianship. Assumptions, practices, and procedures had been accepted, applied, and taught without the benefit of critical examination and clear explanation. But with the opening of the Graduate Library School, a graduate program was inaugurated that gradually changed these conditions.

The Graduate Library School was established to contribute to librarianship what Johns Hopkins University School of Medicine and the Harvard University Law School had contributed to their respective fields. Basic discoveries and systematic advances in medicine were greatly enhanced by the medical research and teaching programs that were introduced at Johns Hopkins, just as the task of administering equal and impartial justice by a capable judiciary was considerably improved by the legal research and teaching programs that were established at Harvard. Established at the University of Chicago, an eminent university that was already widely acclaimed for its promotion of original research and scholarship, the Graduate Library School commenced a program designed to earn a place among first-rate schools and to fulfill the expectations of those responsible for its establishment. Accordingly, the faculty of the school stated that:

1. The most important single responsibility of the School is to meet the standards of scholarship and research maintained by other graduate departments of the University, both in the character of work undertaken by the staff and by the research interests of its graduates.
2. The major aim is research, defined as "extending the existing body of factual knowledge concerning the values and procedures of libraries in their many aspects, and including the development of methods of investigation whereby significant data are obtained, tested, and applied."
3. The School allows other library schools to assume the responsibility for passing on to their students a body of principles and practices that have been found useful in the conduct of libraries. Such training is not a function of this School, but is an essential prerequisite for admission. . . .[24]

This bold, new library education program was based on the proposition that there was as yet no science of librarianship and that such a body of knowledge could only be created by systematic and disciplined research and scholarship.[25] The program was designed to study librarianship by subjecting it to exact observations, precise explanations, and critical evaluations; it was a program that was to be guided by the principles of scientific research. Hence, in substance and approach, the program was a complete departure from established methods of educating librarians.

The new library education program was enthusiastically greeted by some not only as a correct approach to the establishment of fundamental principles in librarianship, but also as an approach based on the same scientific method that was being widely and successfully employed in other professions.[26] Indeed, Charles C. Williamson, dean of the Columbia University School of Library Service, stated that:

If the library is to rise to its opportunity as a social institution and educational force it must begin very soon to attack its problems by a thoroughgoing application of the spirit and methods of research that are being found so effective in every other field. In the natural sciences as well as in the humanistic and social sciences, in the applied sciences, in education, in business and industry, in social service—everywhere except in the library field—extensive programs of research are being carried out, highly organized and well financed.[27]

In addition to the fears already discussed, and despite Williamson's plea, a confusion developed concerning the nature and purpose of scientific method and research. To dispel the confusion, Pierce Butler, a member of the faculty of the Graduate Library School wrote an essay. Addressing it not to research workers, "but to busy practitioners in the hope of winning their sympathetic understanding of the attempt now under way to establish this necessary library science," Butler emphasized his appeal for a sympathetic understanding with clarity and perception. He declared:

Not every librarian is called to take active part in the synthesis of library science. While a few are pursuing such studies the many must continue to devote their whole strength to the normal functions and growth of the established library system. But it is of the utmost importance that every library worker should have a sympathetic understanding of what is being attempted. Only thus is there any assurance that the resultant science will take into account every phase of librarianship that is amenable to scientific treatment, and only thus will its purely humanistic phases be preserved intact as a part of professional practice.[28]

After defining and describing the nature of science and the scientific method, Butler isolated and analyzed some sociological, psychological, and historical problems of librarianship, demonstrating that very little factual information existed in these areas. He also stated that many aspects of these problems could be subjected to the "ruthless" scrutiny of the scientific method without any loss of the humanistic qualities of librarianship, of which many librarians were fearful. Of equal importance, he urged that only through similar critical study of all unexamined basic assumptions of librarianship could there be developed a systematic body of knowledge about librarianship—a library science.

While Butler did not dispel all of the confusion that accompanied the Graduate Library School's effort to create a library science by using the scientific method of research,[29] he undoubtedly removed some of the misunderstandings and helped the school to continue to enrich its program and attract promising students, nine of whom had received the Ph.D. degree by 1939.[30]

But probably his most important accomplishment was in helping to show that the spirit of scientific research and graduate study had emerged as powerful forces and were giving new direction to the course of development of education for librarianship in 1939.

CONCLUSIONS

Education for librarianship, by 1939, had reached a significant stage of development which sharply contrasted with its status of 1919. Its improvement was the result of interaction between the forces and movements which have been analyzed and discussed in this study. These forces and movements possessed enormous potentials for constructiveness and could have been used not only to improve existent library education, but also to develop a system of library education which was capable of providing librarians for all types of library work as well as one which was capable of modifications in order to meet future needs. But these potentials were not fully exploited because the forces and movements often operated without the benefit of an agency with sufficient power to coordinate and use them to develop an articulated library education system.

At the first postwar meeting of the American Library Association, critical attention was focused on the acute shortage of adequately trained librarians for all types of library work and the inability of the training agencies to supply them. Recognition of the personnel shortage and the inadequacies of the library schools led to a series of activities which culminated in the creation of the Board of Education for Librarianship in 1924.

The Board of Education for Librarianship was created to improve the quality of library education by standardizing and accrediting library training agencies, and it was also responsible for increasing the opportunities for obtaining adequate and appropriate library training by securing more financial aid for students, teachers, and library schools. Although many of the chaotic conditions in library education which confronted the board in 1924 had been removed by 1939, it had not succeeded in removing the inadequacies which existed in training for school and special librarians. Indeed, the problem of providing professional education for school and special librarians had become more complex by 1939, and a solution to it appeared beyond the powers of the board with its limited control over the teachers colleges and AALS. This lack of control over the agencies which were capable of developing library education programs for school and special librarians further focuses attention on the absence of an agency with sufficient power to coordinate the various library training programs.

The more than $4 million which the Carnegie Corporation gave to improve library education and to increase the opportunities for obtaining it were extremely helpful, but they also had a restricting effect on efforts to expand the library education curriculum. The principal defender of the traditional concept of library education was AALS, which held that the first year of library schooling should only be devoted to training general librarians, and that no part of it should be devoted to training for specific library positions. By adhering to this concept, AALS increased the complexity of the problem of providing library training for school and special librarians. Since more than $1 million of the corporation's Ten-Year Program in Library Service was used to support the library schools that were members of AALS, the corporation indirectly undermined its own efforts to improve and expand library education.

On the other hand, the Ten-Year Program in Library Service did provide for the establishment of the Graduate Library School of the University of Chicago which set new standards in library education. The Graduate Library School's curriculum, with its strong emphasis on the scientific method and basic research, engendered some severe criticism during the thirties. Some critical questions were asked not only about the value and content of the Graduate Library School's curriculum, but also about the need for library training at all. While none of these questions had been satisfactorily answered even by 1939, it was clear by then that the Graduate Library School was emerging as a strong influence on the course of development of library education and was channeling it into new directions.

Notes

CHAPTER 1

1. William J. McGlothin, *The Professional Schools* (New York: Center for Applied Research in Education, Inc., 1964), pp. 1-5.

2. William Frederick Norwood, *Medical Education in the United States before the Civil War* (Philadelphia; Univ. of Pennsylvania Pr., 1944), p. 380.

3. John S. Brubacher and Willis Rudy, *Higher Education in Transition* (New York: Harper & Brothers, 1958), pp. 199-200.

4. Norwood, p. 381.

5. Brubacher and Rudy, p. 200.

6. Daniel C. Gilman, *Nineteenth Annual Report of the President of the Johns Hopkins University* (Baltimore: Johns Hopkins Pr., 1894), pp. 13-17.

7. Abraham Flexner, *Medical Education in the United States and Canada* (Boston: Merrymount Pr. 1910).

8. Herman Oliphant, "Parallels in the Development of Legal and Medical Education," *The Annals of the American Academy of Political and Social Sciences* 167:157 (May 1933); Lloyd E. Blaugh, ed., *Education for the Professions* (Washington, D.C.: Gov. Print. Off., 1955), p. 112; Brubacher and Rudy, pp. 196-202.

9. Louis R. Wilson, "Aspects of Education for Librarianship in America," *Library Quarterly* 2:1-10 (Jan. 1932).

10. Tse-Chien Tai, *Professional Education for Librarianship* (New York: Wilson, 1925), p. vi.

11. Sarah K. Vann, *Training for Librarianship before 1923* (Chicago: American Library Assn., 1961), p. 1.

12. Carl M. White, *The Origin of the American Library School* (New York: Scarecrow, 1961), p. 7.

13. Bernard Berelson, ed., *Education for Librarianship* (Chicago: American Library Assn., 1949), p. 44.

CHAPTER 2

1. William W. Bishop, "President's Address: The American Library Association at the Crossroads," *ALA Bulletin* 13:100 (July 1919).

2. Ibid, p. 101.

3. A. H. Shearer, "Historical Sketch of the Library War Service," *ALA Bulletin* 13:224 (July 1919).

4. Bishop, "President's Address," p. 101.

5. Carl H. Milan, "American Library Association War Service: Statement by Acting General Director as to Operations," *ALA Bulletin* 13:201 (July 1919).

6. Shearer, "Historical Sketch," pp. 226, 229.

7. American Library Association, "Annual Report of Committee on Committees," *ALA Bulletin* 17:179 (July 1923).

8. "Conference Proceedings of the American Library Association, June 22–27, 1908," *ALA Bulletin* 2:202 (Sept. 1908).

9. "Conference Proceedings of the American Library Association, June 26–July 3, 1909," *ALA Bulletin* 3:442 (Sept. 1909).

10. Phineas L. Windsor, "The Association of American Library Schools," *ALA Bulletin* 11:160–61 (July 1917).

11. Ibid., p. 161.

12. "Conference Proceedings of the American Library Association, June 23–27, 1919," *ALA Bulletin* 13:395 (July 1919).

13. Andrew Keogh, "Advanced Library Training for Research Workers," *ALA Bulletin* 13:165–67 (July 1919).

14. Sarah C. N. Bogle, "Training for High School Librarianship," *ALA Bulletin* 13:277 (July 1919).

15. Mary E. Robbins, "Training Teacher-Librarians in Normal Schools," *ALA Bulletin* 13:279 (July 1919).

16. J. H. Friedel, "Training for Librarianship," *"Library Journal* 44:572–73 (Sept. 1919); Arthur D. Little, "Chemistry and the Special Library—A Foreword," *Special Libraries* 10:86 (May 1919).

17. Frank K. Walter, "Training for the Librarians of a Business Library or a Business Branch," *ALA Bulletin* 13:275–76 (July 1919).

18. "Report of the Committee on the Higher Education of Librarians" (1919), *Papers and Proceedings of the American Library Institute*, p. 233.

19. New England Librarians, "Committee on Graduate Training of College Library Assistants," *Papers and Proceedings of the American Library Institute*, pp. 236–41 (1919).

20. Charles C. Williamson, "The Need of a Plan for Library Development," *Library Journal* 43:649–55 (Sept. 1918).

21. Charles C. Williamson, "Some Present–Day Aspects of Library Training," *ALA Bulletin* 13:120 (July 1919).

22. Ibid., p. 121.

23. Ibid., p. 120.

24. Emma Baldwin, "The Education of Librarians," *Papers and Proceedings of the American Library Institute*, pp. 226–32 (1919).

25. Ibid., p. 229.

26. Ibid., pp. 230–31.

27. American Library Association, "Special A.L.A. Conference," *ALA Bulletin* 14:78 (Jan. 1920).

28. American Library Association, "Report of the Special Committee on Certification, Standardization, and Library Training," *ALA Bulletin* 14:311 (July 1920).

29. Ibid., p. 313.

30. American Library Association, "Council, First Session," *ALA Bulletin* 14:323–24 (July 1920).

31. American Library Association, "Committee Reports: National Certification and Training," *ALA Bulletin* 15:79 (Jan.–Nov. 1921).

32. Ibid., p. 83.

33. American Library Association, "Report of Committee on Library Training," *ALA Bulletin* 14:284 (July 1920).

34. American Library Association, "Committee Reports: Library Training," *ALA Bulletin* 15:66 (Jan.–Nov. 1921).

35. J. H. Friedel, "Aces for Librarianship," *Special Libraries* 11:15–17 (Jan. 1920).

36. Ibid.

37. "Constitution of the Library Workers' Association," *Library Journal* 45:839–40 (Oct. 15, 1920).

38. Catherine Van Dyne, "Why a Library Workers' Association?" *Library Journal* 46:939–40 (Nov. 15, 1921).

39. "The Library Workers' Association," *Library Journal* 45:219 (Mar. 1, 1920).

40. "Recruiting for Librarianship," *Library Journal* 46:859–60 (Oct. 1921).

41. American Library Association, "Committee Reports: Library Training," *ALA Bulletin* 17:195–96 (July 1923).

42. Ibid., 15:68 (Jan.–Nov. 1921).

43. Ibid., 16:207–8 (July 1922).

44. American Library Association, "Council: First Session," *ALA Bulletin* 16:149–50 (July 1922).

45. American Library Association, "Committee Reports: Library Training," *ALA Bulletin* 17:195 (July 1923).

46. American Library Association, "Council: First and Second Sessions," *ALA Bulletin* 17:152–53 (July 1923).

47. "Editorial," *Library Journal* 49–129 (Feb. 1, 1924).

48. "What the Temporary Library Training Board Is Doing," *ALA Bulletin* 18:5–7 (Jan. 1924).

49. Ibid.

50. Ibid., p. 6–7.

51. "Editorial," *ALA Bulletin* 18:113 (May 1924).

52. "Meetings in New York City," *Public Libraries* 19:246–47 (May 1924).

53. "Conference on Library Training," *Library Journal* 49:425 (May 1, 1924).

54. "Meetings in New York City," p. 246.

55. "Editorial," *Library Journal* 49:428–49 (May 1, 1924).

56. "Report of the Temporary Training Board," *ALA Bulletin* 18:258 (Aug. 1924).

57. Ibid., pp. 258–59.

58. Ibid.

59. American Library Association, "Papers and Proceedings," *ALA Bulletin* 18:197–99 (Aug. 1924).

60. "Board of Education for Librarianship," *ALA Bulletin* 18:125 (July 1924).

CHAPTER 3

1. George B. Utley, "The Expanding Responsibilities of the American Library Association," *ALA Bulletin* 17:111 (July 1923).

2. American Library Association, "Papers and Proceedings," *ALA Bulletin* 17:199 (July 1923).

3. Utley, p. 111.

4. American Library Association, "Papers and Proceedings," *ALA Bulletin* 19:227–28 (July 1925).

5. Ibid.

6. Ibid., p. 231.

7. Ibid., pp. 231–32.

8. Harriet E. Howe, "Two Decades of Education for Librarianship," *Library Quarterly* 12: 557–70 (July 1942).

9. American Library Association, "Papers and Proceedings," *ALA Bulletin* 19:233 (July 1925).

10. Ibid., pp. 235–36.

11. Howe, p. 563.

12. Association of American Library Schools, "Minutes and Proceedings, 1923," mimeographed (Library, Graduate Library School, Univ. of Illinois), pp. 20–27.

13. Association of American Universities, "Report of the Committee on Academic and Professional Higher Degrees," *Journal of Proceedings* 26: 25–26 (Oct. 31–Nov. 1, 1924).

14. American Library Association, "Papers and Proceedings," *ALA Bulletin* 19:235 (July 1925).

15. Ibid., pp. 160–62.

16. American Library Association, "Papers and Proceedings," *ALA Bulletin* 11:277–92 (July 1917).

17. Jessie Wells, "Secondary Education in Library Work," *ALA Bulletin* 11: 148 (July 1917).

18. American Library Association, "Papers and Proceedings," *ALA Bulletin* 20: 432 (Oct. 1926).

19. Ibid., pp. 430–31.

20. Ibid., pp. 429–30.

21. Charles E. Rush, "Proposed Regional Library Training Courses," *ALA Bulletin* 19:326 (July 1925).

22. American Library Association, "Minimum Standards for Summer Courses in Library Science," *ALA Bulletin* 20:23 (Feb. 1926).

23. American Library Association, "Papers and Proceedings," *ALA Bulletin* 20:431 (Oct. 1926).

24. Ibid., pp. 438–59.

25. American Library Association, "Minimum Standards for Curricula in School Library Work," *ALA Bulletin* 20:341–42 (Oct. 1926).

26. Charles C. Williamson, *Training for Library Service*, a report prepared for the Carnegie Corporation (Boston: Merrymount Pr., 1923).

27. Ibid., p. 25.

28. Ibid., p. 49.

29. American Library Association, "Papers and Proceedings," *ALA Bulletin* 20:421 (Oct. 1926).

30. "Institute for Instructors in Library Science," *Public Libraries* 32:146 (Mar. 1927).

31. "Library Schools: University of Chicago," *Public Libraries* 31:421–22 (Oct. 1926); American Library Association, "Papers and Proceedings," *ALA Bulletin* 21:394–95 (Oct. 1927).

32. Board of Education for Librarianship, "Curriculum Study," *ALA Bulletin* 19:47 (Nov. 1925).

33. American Library Association, "Papers and Proceedings," *ALA Bulletin* 20:439–40 (Oct. 1926).

34. W. W. Charters, "Job Analysis in Education for Librarianship," *Public Libraries* 32:7–10 (Jan. 1927).

35. American Library Association, "Annual Reports: Fourth Annual Report of the Board of Education for Librarianship," *ALA Bulletin* 22:169 (June 1928).

36. American Library Association, "Annual Reports: Sixth Annual Report of the Board of Education for Librarianship," *ALA Bulletin* 24:176 (May 1930).

37. Ibid., p. 177.

38. Ibid., p. 191.

39. American Library Association, "The Seventh Annual Report of the Board of Education for Librarianship" *ALA Bulletin* 25:191 (Apr. 1931).

40. Carnegie Corporation of New York, *Report of Informal Conferences on Library Interests* (New York, 1931), p. 32. The report is in the collection of the Library School of the Univ. of Illinois.

41. Julia W. Merrill, "The Challenge of the Depression," *ALA Bulletin* 25: 703–7 (Dec. 1931).

42. James I. Wyer, "Unemployment among Librarians," *ALA Bulletin* 26: 703–7 (Dec. 1931).

43. "Unemployment and Salaries," *Proceedings of the American Library Association* (1933), p. 811.

44. "Unemployment in the Profession," *ALA Bulletin* 26:87–90 (Feb. 1932).

45. "Salaries and Unemployment," *ALA Bulletin* 27:93–98 (Jan. 1933).

46. "Unemployment and Salaries," *Proceedings of the American Library Association* (1933), p. 811.

47. Rebecca B. Rankin, "Unemployment Among Librarians," *ALA Bulletin* 29:148–50 (May 1935).

48. "Salaries, Staff, and Service," *ALA Bulletin* 31:602–3 (Sept. 1937).

49. American Library Association, "Annual Reports: Third Annual Report of the Board of Education for Librarianship," *ALA Bulletin* 21:183 (July 1927).

50. American Library Association, "Annual Reports: Fifth Annual Report of the Board of Education for Librarianship," *ALA Bulletin* 23:154 (June 1929).

51. Ibid.

52. "Sixth Annual Report of the Board of Education for Librarianship," p. 177.

53. Association of American Library Schools, "Proceedings," Dec. 1931, mimeographed (Library, Graduate Library School, Univ. of Illinois), p. 3.

54. "Annual Reports: Seventh Annual Report of the Board of Education for Librarianship," p. 197.

55. "Unemployment among Librarians," *ALA Bulletin* 27:178 (Mar. 1932).

56. American Library Association, "Annual Reports: Ninth Annual Report of the Board of Education for Librarianship," *ALA Bulletin* 27:429 (Oct. 1933).

57. Association of American Library Schools, "Proceedings," Apr. 1932, mimeographed (Library, Graduate School, Univ. of Illinois), p. 6.

58. C. B. Joeckel, "Supply and Demand in the Library Profession," mimeographed (*Proceedings of the American Association of Library Schools*, Exhibit A, Dec. 1931) pp. 1–10; R. A. Miller, "Unemployment and the Library Schools," *ALA Bulletin* 27:221–22 (May 1933).

59. "The Open Round Table," *Library Journal* 58:314 (Apr. 1, 1933).

60. Miller, p. 221.

61. B. E. Hodges, "Unemployment Prevention and Re-employment," *ALA Bulletin* 30:93 (Feb. 1936).

CHAPTER 4

1. Carnegie Corporation of New York, *Proposed Program in Library Service*, Office Memorandum, November 10, 1925 (New York, 1925), p. 1. The report is in the collection of the library school of the Univ. of Illinois.

2. Robert M. Lester, *Review of Grants for Library Interests, 1911-1935*, Printed for the Information of the Trustees of the Carnegie Corporation (New York, 1935), p. 123. The report is in the collection of the library school of the Univ. of Illinois.

3. Ibid.

4. Ibid.

5. Ibid., pp. 125–26.

6. Supra, chap. 2, p. 11.

7. Charles C. Williamson, *Training for Library Service*, a report prepared for the Carnegie Corporation of New York (Boston: Merrymount Pr., 1923).

8. Ibid., chap. 19.

9. Charles C. Williamson, "The Need of a Plan for Library Development," *Library Journal* 43:649 (Sept. 1918).

10. Wilhelm Munthe, *American Librarianship from a European Angle* (Chicago: American Library Assn., 1939), p. 132.

11. "The Williamson Report: Comments from the Library Schools," *Library Journal* 48:899–900 (Jan. 1, 1923).

12. Ibid., pp. 900–2.

13. "The Williamson Report—II: Comments from Librarians," *Library Journal* 48:1001 (Dec. 1, 1923).

14. "The Williamson Report: Comments from the Library Schools," *Library Journal* 48:902 (Jan. 1, 1923).

15. Ibid., pp. 902–3.

16. Ibid., pp. 903–4.

17. Ibid., pp. 904–5.

18. Ibid., p. 905.

19. Ibid.

20. Ibid., p. 906.

21. Ibid., p. 907.

22. Ibid.

23. Ibid., p. 909.

24. Ibid., p. 910.

25. Ibid.

26. "The Williamson Report—II: Comments from Librarians," *Library Journal* 48:999 (Dec. 1, 1923).

27. Ibid., p. 1002.

28. Edwin H. Anderson, "Training for Library Service," *Library Journal* 49:463 (May 1924).

29. "The Williamson Report—II," p. 1005.

30. Ibid.

31. Anderson, pp. 462–66.

32. Williamson, *Training for Library Service*, p. 122.

33. American Library Association, "Committee Reports: Library Training," *ALA Bulletin* 18:237–38 (Aug. 1924).

34. Lester, p. 126.

35. Adam Strohm, "The Library Training Board," *ALA Bulletin* 18:3 (Jan. 1924).

36. Lester, p. 127.

37. Carnegie Corporation of New York, "Resolution B–367: Ten-Year Program in Library Service," *Report of the President and Treasurer, 1925*, p. 47. The report is in the collection of the library school of the Univ. of Illinois.

38. Ray Trautman, *A History of the School of Library Service, Columbia University* (New York: Columbia Univ. Pr., 1954), p. 27.

39. Ibid.

40. Charles C. Williamson, *Annual Report of the Director of the School of Library Service*, Columbia University Information Bulletin, 1927, p. 4.

41. *Library School of the New York Public Library: Register, 1911–1926* (New York: The New York Public Library, 1929), pp. 9–10.

42. Ibid.

43. Trautman, p. 33.

44. *Library School of the New York Public Library: Register*, p. 10.

45. *Papers and Proceedings of the American Library Institute*, pp. 236–39.

46. "Board of Education for Librarianship," *ALA Bulletin* 19:6 (Jan. 1925).

47. Association of American Universities, "Report of the Committee on Academic and Professional Higher Degrees," *Journal of Proceedings* 26: 25–26 (Oct. 31–Nov. 1, 1924).

48. "Board of Education for Librarianship," *ALA Bulletin* 19:5, 17 (Jan. 1925).

49. Ibid., p. 246.

50. Robert M. Lester, *New Frontiers in Librarianship*, Proceedings of the special meeting of the American Association of Library Schools and the Board of Education for Librarianship of the American Library Association in honor of the University of Chicago and the Graduate Library School (Chicago: Univ. of Chicago Pr., 1940), p. 26.

51. Ibid.

52. Frederick P. Keppel, "The Carnegie Corporation and the Graduate Library School: A Historical Outline," *Library Quarterly* 1:23 (Jan. 1931).

53. Carnegie Corporation of New York, *Proposed Program in Library Service . . .* , p. 3.

54. Keppel, p. 23.

55. Ibid., p. 25.

56. Carnegie Corporation, *Proposed Program in Library Service . . .* , p. 1.

57. William S. Learned, *The American Public Library and the Diffusion of Knowledge* (New York: Harcourt, 1924).

58. Ibid., p. 77.

59. Ibid., p. 75.

60. Ibid., p. 76.

61. Ibid., p. 80.

CHAPTER 5

1. Association of American Library Schools, "Minutes of the Meeting Held December 29, 1928." mimeographed (Chicago, Ill.), p. 1.

2. Association of American Library Schools, "Minutes of the Meeting Held May 13, 1929," mimeographed (Washington, D.C.), pp. 3–4.

3. Ibid., p. 6.

4. Association of American Library Schools, "Proceedings," Dec. 30, 1929, mimeographed (Library, Graduate Library School, Univ. of Illinois), p. 5.

5. J. C. Dana, "Letter to the Members of the Executive Board of the A.L.A.," *ALA Bulletin* 23:13 (Jan. 1929).

6. "Board of Education for Librarianship," *ALA Bulletin* 24:621 (Dec. 1930).

7. Ibid., p. 623.

8. Ibid.

9. Ibid., pp. 621–22.

10. Ibid., p. 623.

11. Louis R. Wilson, "The Board of Education for Librarianship," *ALA Bulletin* 25:5–11 (Jan. 1931).

12. Carnegie Corporation of New York, *Report of Informal Conferences on Library Interests* (New York, 1931), p. 38. The report is in the collection of the library school of the Univ. of Illinois.

13. Ibid., p. 10.

14. Association of American Library Schools, "Minutes of Meeting Held May 13, 1929," pp. 3–4.

15. Association of American Library Schools, "Proceedings," June 24–25, 1931, mimeographed (Library, Graduate Library School, Univ. of Illinois), p. 3.

16. Association of American Library Schools, "Proceedings," Dec. 29, 1930, mimeographed (Library, Graduate Library School, Univ. of Illinois), p. 5.

17. Wilson, p. 9.

18. Edith M. Coulter, "The Future of the Association of American Library Schools" mimeographed (American Association of Library Schools Report of May 10, 1936, meeting, Richmond, Va.), p. 1.

19. Ralph Munn, "The Objectives of the Association of American Library Schools" mimeographed (American Association of Library Schools Report of May 10, 1936, meeting, p. 5.

20. American Library Association, "Annual Reports: First Annual Report of the Board of Education for Librarianship," *ALA Bulletin* 19:227–28 (July 1925).

21. American Library Association, "Minimum Standards for Curricula in School Library Work," *ALA Bulletin* 20:419 (Oct. 1926).

22. American Library Association, "Annual Reports: Fifth Annual Report of the Board of Education for Librarianship," *ALA Bulletin* 23:154 (June 1929).

23. William F. Russell, "The School Librarian Situation," *School and Society* 24:113–18 (July 1926).

24. Ibid., p. 115.

25. Ibid.

26. "Standard Library Organization and Equipment for Secondary Schools of Different Sizes," *Addresses and Proceedings of the National Education Association,* 56:691–719 (1918).

27. Ibid., pp. 699–70.

28. Ibid., p. 700.

29. Lucile Fargo, *Preparation for School Library Work* (New York: Columbia Univ. Pr., 1936), p. 51.

30. C. C. Certain, "Report of the Joint Committee on Elementary School Library Standards," *Bulletin of the Department of Elementary School Principals* 4:326–59 (July 1925).

31. Ibid., p. 337.

32. American Library Association, "Annual Reports: Third Annual Report of the Board of Education for Librarianship," *ALA Bulletin* 21:181 (July 1927).

33. American Library Association, "Annual Reports: Sixth Annual Report of the Board of Education for Librarianship," *ALA Bulletin* 24:182 (May 1930).

34. Robbins, p. 279.

35. American Library Association Education Committee, *School Library Yearbook Number 4* (Chicago: American Library Assn., 1931), pp. 116–26.

36. "Certification—A Summary," *ALA Bulletin* 30:886 (Sept. 1936).

37. "Standard Library Organization and Equipment for Accredited Secondary Schools of Different Sizes," *Proceedings of the North Central Association of Colleges and Secondary Schools*, pp. 44–77 (1918).

38. *School Library Yearbook Number 4*, pp. 101–08.

39. "Standards for Secondary Schools: Standards for School Libraries," *Proceedings of the Association of Colleges and Secondary Schools of the Southern States* 35:286 (1930).

40. D. S. Campbell, *Libraries in the Accredited High Schools of the Association of Colleges and Secondary Schools of the Southern States. A Report of the Status of High School Libraries with Respect to the New Library Standards of the Association.* (Nashville, 1930), p. 8.

41. Joint Committee of the American Association of Teachers' Colleges and the American Library Association, *How Shall We Educate Teachers and Librarians for Library Service in the School?* (New York: Columbia Univ. Pr., 1936).

42. Ernest J. Reece, *The Curriculum in Library Schools* (New York: Columbia Univ. Pr., 1936), pp. 8–9.

43. Rebecca B. Rankin, "Training for the Special Librarian," *Special Libraries* 17:329 (Nov. 1926).

44. Rebecca B. Rankin, "Training for Special Librarians," *Special Libraries* 18:226 (Sept. 1927).

45. Ibid.

46. Rankin, "Training for the Special Librarian," pp. 329–30.

47. James I. Wyer, "The Training of the Special Librarian," *Special Libraries* 23:342 (Sept. 1932).

48. Ibid.

49. Harriett E. Howe, "What Training for Special Librarians?" *Special Libraries* 29:216 (Sept. 1938).

50. Margaret G. Smith, "Why and What Are Special Librarians?" *Special Libraries* 28:144 (May–June 1937).

51. J. H. Shera, "Training for Specials': The Status of the Library Schools," *Special Libraries* 28:320 (Nov. 1937).

52. June R. Donnelly, "Library Training for the Special Librarian," *Special Libraries* 12:186–88 (Sept.–Oct. 1921).

53. J. H. Shera, "Training for Specials: A Prologue to Revision," *Special Libraries* 28:143 (May–June 1937).

54. Howe, "What Training for Special Librarians?"

55. Harriett E. Howe, "The First-Year Library-School Curriculum" in *Library Trends*, ed. Louis R. Wilson (Chicago: Univ. of Chicago Pr., 1936), pp. 361–74.

56. Ernest J. Reece, *Some Possible Developments in Library Education* (Chicago: American Library Assn., 1924).

57. Ibid., p. 14.

58. Association of American Library Schools, "Report of Meeting," June 13, 1938, mimeographed (Kansas City, Kan.), p. 1.

59. Ethel M. Fair, "Professional Training for Special Librarians," *Proceedings of the Special Libraries Association*, pp. 5–7 (1939).

CHAPTER 6

1. Carnegie Corporation of New York, *Report of Informal Conferences . . .* , p. 43.

2. "Board of Education for Librarianship," *ALA Bulletin* 24:623.

3. F. J. Kelly, "Report on Standardizing Agencies," *Transactions and Proceedings of the National Association of State Universities: Part II*, 24:114 (Nov. 15–16, 1926).

4. Carnegie Corporation of New York, *Report of Informal Conferences . . .* , p. 43.

5. American Library Association, "Annual Reports: Fourth Annual Report of the Board of Education for Librarianship," p. 168.

6. Wilson, "The Board of Education for Librarianship," p. 9–10.

7. "Revisions of Minimum Standards," *ALA Buletin* 24:180–81 (May 1930).

8. American Library Association, "Annual Reports: Ninth Annual Report of the Board of Education for Librarianship," p. 429.

9. "Council; Second Session: Minimum Requirements for Library Schools," *ALA Bulletin* 27:613 (Dec. 1933).

10. Ibid., p. 429.

11. Ibid., p. 610.

12. Ibid.

13. Association of American Library Schools, "Minutes and Proceedings, 1923," pp. 20–27.

14. Association of American Universities, "Report of the Committee on Academic and Professional Higher Degrees," pp. 25–26.

15. Columbia University, *Report of the Director of the School of Library Service, 1929* (New York: Columbia Univ. Pr., 1929), p. 10.

16. Ralph Munn, *Conditions and Trends in Education for Librarianship*, a report on the Program in Training for Library Service Adopted by the Board of Trustees of Carnegie Corporation of New York, March 19, 1926, together with the Report of Committee on Library Training, November, 1934, and other documents. "Report of the Committee Convened, April, 1933, by the Carnegie Corporation to Study Trends in Education for Librarianship" (Carnegie Corporation of New York, 1936), p. 35.

17. Ibid., p. 39.

18. Ibid., p. 17.

19. C. Seymour Thompson, "Do We Want a Library Science?" *Library Journal* 56:581 (July 1931).

20. Munn, p. 45.

21. Ibid., p. 17.

22. Ibid., p. 20.

23. Ibid., p. 47.

24. Douglas Waples, "The Graduate Library School at Chicago," *Library Quarterly* 1:26–27 (Jan. 1931).

25. Thompson, p. 581.

26. Carl B. Roden, "President's Address: Ten Years," *ALA Bulletin* 22:315 (Sept. 1928).

27. Charles C. Williamson, "The Place of Research in Library Service," *Library Quarterly* 1:3 (Jan. 1931).

28. Pierce Butler, *An Introduction to Library Science* (Chicago: Univ. of Chicago Pr., 1933), pp. xiv–xv.

29. Leon Carnovsky, "Why Graduate Study in Librarianship?" *Library Quarterly* 7:246 (Apr. 1937).

30. American Library Association, *Final Report of the Committee on Fellowships and Scholarships of the American Library Association, October 1, 1942* (Chicago: American Library Assn., 1943).

Bibliography

BOOKS

American Library Association Education Committee. *School Library Yearbook Number 4.* Chicago: American Library Assn., 1931.

Berelson, Bernard, ed. *Education for Librarianship.* Chicago: American Library Assn., 1949.

Blaugh, Lloyd E., ed. *Education for the Professions.* Washington, D.C.: Govt. Print. Off., 1955.

Brubacher, John S., and Rudy, Willis. *Higher Education in Transition.* New York: Harper & Brothers, 1958.

Butler, Pierce. *An Introduction to Library Science.* Chicago: Univ. of Chicago, Pr., 1933.

Columbia University. *Report of the Director of the School of Library Service, 1929.* New York: Columbia Univ. Pr., 1929.

Fargo, Lucile. *Preparation for School Library Work.* New York: Columbia Univ. Pr., 1936.

Flexner, Abraham. *Medical Education in the United States and Canada.* Boston: Merrymount Pr., 1910.

Gilman, Daniel C. *Nineteenth Annual Report of the President of the Johns Hopkins University.* Baltimore: Johns Hopkins Pr., 1894.

Howe, Harriett E. "The First-Year Library-School Curriculum" in *Library Trends*. Edited by Louis R. Wilson. Chicago: Univ. of Chicago Pr., 1936.

Joint Committee of the American Association of Teachers' Colleges and the American Library Association. *How Shall We Educate Teachers and Librarians for Library Service in the School?* New York: Columbia Univ. Pr., 1936.

Learned, William S. *The American Public Library and the Diffusion of Knowledge*. New York: Harcourt, 1924.

McGlothin, William J. *The Professional Schools*. New York: Center for Applied Research in Education, Inc., 1964.

Munthe, Wilhelm. *American Librarianship from a European Angle*. Chicago: American Library Assn., 1939.

Norwood, William Frederick. *Medical Education in the United States before the Civil War*. Philadelphia: Univ. of Pennsylvania Pr., 1944.

Reece, Ernest J. *The Curriculum in Library Schools*. New York: Columbia Univ. Pr., 1936.

———. *Some Possible Developments in Library Education*. Chicago: American Library Assn., 1924.

Tai, Tse-Chien. *Professional Education for Librarianship*. New York: Wilson, 1925.

Trautman, Ray. *A History of the School of Library Service, Columbia University*. New York: Columbia Univ. Pr., 1954.

Vann, Sarah K. *Training for Librarianship before 1923*. Chicago: American Library Assn., 1961.

White, Carl M. *The Origin of the American Library School*. New York: Scarecrow, 1961.

ARTICLES AND PERIODICALS

American Library Association. "Annual Reports: First Annual Report of the Board of Education for Librarianship." *ALA Bulletin* 19:226–63 (July 1925).

———. "Annual Reports: Third Annual Report of the Board of Education for Librarianship." *ALA Bulletin* 21:170–93 (July 1927).

———. "Annual Reports: Fourth Annual Report of the Board of Education for Librarianship." *ALA Bulletin* 22:163–82 (June 1928).

———. "Annual Reports: Fifth Annual Report of the Board of Education for Librarianship." *ALA Bulletin* 23:147–66 (June 1929).

―――. "Annual Reports: Sixth Annual Report of the Board of Education for Librarianship." *ALA Bulletin* 24:175–98 (May 1930).

―――. "Annual Reports: Seventh Annual Report of the Board of Education for Librarianship." *ALA Bulletin* 25:190–217 (May 1931).

―――. "Annual Reports: Ninth Annual Report of the Board of Education for Librarianship." *ALA Bulletin* 27:427–33 (Oct. 1933).

―――. "Annual Report of Committee on Committees." *ALA Bulletin* 17:179–82 (July 1923).

―――. "Committee Reports: Library Training." *ALA Bulletin* 15:78–79 (Jan.–Nov. 1921).

―――. "Committee Reports: Library Training," *ALA Bulletin* 16:206–9 (July 1922).

―――. "Committee Reports: Library Training." *ALA Bulletin* 17:194–96 (July 1923).

―――. "Committee Reports: Library Training." *ALA Bulletin* 18:237–38 (Aug. 1924).

―――. "Council, First Session." *ALA Bulletin* 14:321–24 (July 1920).

―――. "Council, First Session." *ALA Bulletin* 16:149–52 (July 1922).

―――. "Council, First and Second Sessions." *ALA Bulletin* 17:150–55 (July 1923).

―――. "Council, Second Session: Minimum Requirements for Library Schools." *ALA Bulletin* 27:610–16 (Dec. 1933).

―――. "Minimum Standards for Curricula in School Library Work." *ALA Bulletin* 20:419 (Oct. 1926).

―――. "Minimum Standards for Summer Courses in Library Science." *ALA Bulletin* 20:23 (Feb. 1926).

―――. "Papers and Proceedings." *ALA Bulletin* 11:277–92 (July 1917).

―――. "Papers and Proceedings." *ALA Bulletin* 17:198–200 (July 1923).

―――. "Papers and Proceedings." *ALA Bulletin* 18:197–99 (Aug. 1924).

―――. "Papers and Proceedings." *ALA Bulletin* 19:227–35 (July 1925).

―――. "Papers and Proceedings." *ALA Bulletin* 20:405–73 (Oct. 1926).

―――. "Papers and Proceedings." *ALA Bulletin* 21:394–95 (Oct. 1927).

————. "Report of Committee on Library Training." *ALA Bulletin* 14:284–89 (July 1920).

————. "Report of the Special Committee on Certification, Standardization, and Library Training." *ALA Bulletin* 14:311–13 (July 1920).

————. "Special A.L.A. Conference." *ALA Bulletin* 14:1–79 (Jan. 1920).

Anderson, Edwin H. "Training for Library Service." *Library Journal* 49:462–66 (May 1924).

Bishop, William W. "President's Address: The American Library Association at the Crossroads." *ALA Bulletin* 13:99–105 (July 1919).

"Board of Education for Librarianship." *ALA Bulletin* 18:124–25 (July 1924).

"Board of Education for Librarianship." *ALA Bulletin* vol. 19 (Jan. 1925).

"Board of Education for Librarianship." *ALA Bulletin* 24:620–28 (Dec. 1930).

Board of Education for Librarianship. "Curriculum Study." *ALA Bulletin* 19:47 (Nov. 1925).

Bogle, Sarah C. N. "Training for High School Librarianship." *ALA Bulletin* 13:277–78 (July 1919).

Carnovsky, Leon. "Why Graduate Study in Librarianship?" *Library Quarterly* 7:246–61 (Apr. 1937).

Certain, C. C. "Report of the Joint Committee on Elementary School Library Standards." *Bulletin of the Department of Elementary School Principals* 4:326–59 (July 1925).

"Certification—A Summary." *ALA Bulletin* 30:886 (Sept. 1936).

Charters, W. W. "Job Analysis in Education for Librarianship." *Public Libraries* 32:7–10 (Jan. 1927).

"Conference on Library Training." *Library Journal* 49:425–26 (May 1, 1924).

"Conference Proceedings of the American Library Association, June 22–27, 1908," *ALA Bulletin* 2:202 (Sept. 1908).

"Conference Proceedings of the American Library Association, June 26–July 3, 1909," *ALA Bulletin* 3:442 (Sept. 1909).

"Conference Proceedings of the American Library Association, June 23–27, 1919," *ALA Bulletin* 13:395 (July 1919).

"Constitution of the Library Workers' Association." *Library Journal* 45:839–40 (Oct. 15, 1920).

Dana, J. C. "Letter to the Members of the Executive Board of the A.L.A." *ALA Bulletin* 23:13 (Jan. 1929).

Donnelly, June R. "Library Training for the Special Librarian." *Special Libraries* 12:186–88 (Sept.–Oct. 1921).

"Editorial." *ALA Bulletin* 18:113–15 (May 1924).

"Editorial." *Library Journal* 49:129 (Feb. 1, 1924).

"Editorial." *Library Journal* 49:428–29 (May 1, 1924).

Friedel, J. H. "Aces for Librarianship." *Special Libraries* 11:15–17 (Jan. 1920).

———. "Training for Librarianship." *Library Journal* 44:569–74 (Sept. 1919).

Hodges, B. E. "Unemployment Prevention and Re-employment." *ALA Bulletin* 30:93–95 (Feb. 1936).

Howe, Harriett E. "Two Decades of Education for Librarianship." *Library Quarterly* 12:557–70 (July 1942).

———. "What Training for Special Librarians?" *Special Libraries* 29:212–17 (Sept. 1938).

"Institute for Instructors in Library Science." *Public Libraries* 32:146 (Mar. 1927).

Keogh, Andrew. "Advanced Library Training for Research Workers." *ALA Bulletin* 13:165–67 (July 1919).

Keppel, Frederick P. "The Carnegie Corporation and the Graduate Library School: A Historical Outline." *Library Quarterly* 1:22–25 (Jan. 1931).

"Library Schools: University of Chicago." *Public Libraries* 31:421–22 (Oct. 1926).

"The Library Workers' Association." *Library Journal* 45:219 (Mar. 1, 1920).

Little, Arthur D. "Chemistry and the Special Library—A Foreword," *Special Libraries* 10:85–86 (May 1919).

"Meetings in New York City." *Public Libraries* 19:246–48 (May 1924).

Merrill, Julia W. "The Challenge of the Depression." *ALA Bulletin* 25:703–7 (Dec. 1931).

Milan, Carl H. "American Library Association War Service: Statement by Acting General Director as to Operations." *ALA Bulletin* 13:201–14 (July 1919).

Miller, R. A. "Unemployment and the Library Schools." *ALA Bulletin* 27:221–22 (May 1933).

Oliphant, Herman. "Parallels in the Development of Legal and Medical Education." *The Annals of the American Academy of Political and Social Sciences* 167:156–72 (May 1933).

"The Open Round Table." *Library Journal* 58:314–15 (Apr. 1, 1933).

Rankin, Rebecca B. "Training for the Special Librarian." *Special Libraries* 17:329–30 (Nov. 1926).

———. "Training for Special Librarians." *Special Libraries* 18:226–28 (Sept. 1927).

―――. "Unemployment Among Librarians." *ALA Bulletin* 29:148–50 (May 1935).

"Recruiting for Librarianship." *Library Journal* 46:859–60 (Oct. 15, 1921).

"Report of the Temporary Training Board." *ALA Bulletin* 18:257–88 (Aug. 1924).

"Revisions of Minimum Standards." *ALA Bulletin* 24:180–81 (May 1930).

Robbins, Mary E. "Training Teacher-Librarians in Normal Schools." *ALA Bulletin* 13:279–81 (July 1919).

Roden, Carl B. "President's Address: Ten Years." *ALA Bulletin* 22:311–18 (Sept. 1928).

Rush, Charles E. "Proposed Regional Library Training Courses." *ALA Bulletin* 19:326–27 (July 1925).

Russell, William F. "The School Librarian Situation." *School and Society* 24:113–18 (July 1926).

"Salaries and Unemployment." *ALA Bulletin* 27:93–98 (Jan. 1933).

"Salaries, Staff, and Service." *ALA Bulletin* 31:601–04 (Sept. 1937).

Shearer, A. H. "Historical Sketch of the Library War Service." *ALA Bulletin* 13:224–33 (July 1919).

Shera, J. H. "Training for Specials: A Prologue to Revision." *Special Libraries* 28:139–44 (May–June 1937).

―――. "Training for Specials: The Status of the Library Schools." *Special Libraries* 28:317–21 (Nov. 1937).

Smith, Margaret G. "Why and What are Special Librarians?" *Special Libraries* 27:144 (May–June 1937).

Strohm, Adam. "The Library Training Board." *ALA Bulletin* 18:2–4 (Jan. 1924).

Thompson, C. Seymour. "Do We Want A Library Science?" *Library Journal* 56:581–87 (July 1931).

"Unemployment among Librarians." *ALA Bulletin* 27:178 (Mar. 1932).

"Unemployment in the Profession." *ALA Bulletin* 26:87–90 (Feb. 1932).

Utley, George B. "The Expanding Responsibilities of the American Library Association." *ALA Bulletin* 17:107–12 (July 1923).

Van Dyne, Catherine. "Why A Library Workers' Association?" *Library Journal* 46:939–40 (Nov. 15, 1921).

Walter, Frank K. "Training for the Librarians of a Business Library or a Business Branch." *ALA Bulletin* 13:273–76 (July 1919).

Waples, Douglas. "The Graduate Library School at Chicago." *Library Quarterly* 1:26–36 (Jan. 1931).

"What the Temporary Training Board is Doing." *ALA Bulletin* 18: 5–9 (Jan. 1924).

Williamson, Charles C. "Some Present-Day Aspects of Library Training." *ALA Bulletin* 13: 120–26 (July 1919).

———. "The Need of a Plan for Library Development." *Library Journal* 43:649–55 (Sept. 1918).

———. "The Place of Research in Library Service." *Library Quarterly* 1:1–17 (Jan. 1931).

"The Williamson Report: Comments from the Library Schools." *Library Journal* 48:899–910 (Jan. 1, 1923).

"The Williamson Report—II: Comments from Librarians." *Library Journal* 48:999–1006 (Dec. 1, 1923).

Wilson, Louis R. "The American Library School Today." *Library Quarterly* 7:211–45 (Apr. 1937).

———. "Aspects of Education for Librarianship in America." *Library Quarterly* 2:1–10 (Jan. 1932).

———. "The Board of Education for Librarianship." *ALA Bulletin* 25:5–11 (Jan. 1931).

Windsor, Phineas L. "The Association of American Library Schools." *ALA Bulletin* 11:160–62 (July 1917).

Wyer, James I. "The Training of the Special Librarian." *Special Libraries* 23:339–44 (Sept. 1932).

———. "Unemployment among Librarians." *ALA Bulletin* 26:22–26 (Jan. 1932).

ADDRESSES, PAPERS AND PROCEEDINGS

Association of American Universities. "Report of the Committee on Academic and Professional Higher Degrees." *Journal of Proceedings* 26 (Oct. 31–Nov. 1, 1924).

Baldwin, Emma. "The Education of Librarians." *Papers and Proceedings of the American Library Institute*, 1919.

Fair, Ethel M. "Professional Training for Special Librarians." *Proceedings of the Special Libraries Association*, 1939.

Kelly, F. J. "Report on Standardizing Agencies." *Transactions and Proceedings of the National Association of State Universities: Part II* 24 (Nov. 15–16, 1926).

Lester, Robert M. *New Frontiers in Librarianship.* Proceedings of the special meeting of the American Association of Library Schools and the Board of Education for Librarianship of the American Library Association in honor of the University of Chicago and the Graduate Library School. Chicago: Univ. of Chicago Pr., 1940.

New England Librarians. "Committee on Graduate Training of College Library Assistants." *Papers and Proceedings of the American Library Institute,* 1919.

"Report of the Committee on the Higher Education of Librarians." *Papers and Proceedings of the American Library Institute,* 1919.

"Standard Library Organization and Equipment for Accredited Secondary Schools of Different Sizes." *Proceedings of the North Central Association of Colleges and Secondary Schools,* 1918.

"Standard Library Organization and Equipment for Secondary Schools of Different Sizes." *Addresses and Proceedings of the National Education Association* 56 (1918).

"Standards for Secondary Schools: Standards for School Libraries." *Proceedings of the Association of Colleges and Secondary Schools of the Southern States* 35 (1930).

"Unemployment and Salaries." *Proceedings of the American Library Association,* 1933.

REPORTS

American Library Association. *Final Report of the Committee On Fellowships and Scholarships of the American Library Association, October 1, 1942.* Chicago: American Library Assn., 1943.

Campbell, D. S. *Libraries in the Accredited High Schools of the Association of Colleges and Secondary Schools of the Southern States.* A report of the Status of High School Libraries with Respect to the New Library Standards of the Association. Nashville, 1930.

Carnegie Corporation of New York. *Proposed Program in Library Service,* Office Memorandum, November 10, 1925. New York, 1925. Publisher not listed. Imprint is Carnegie Corp., 525 N. 5th Ave., New York, N.Y.

————. *Report of Informal Conference on Library Interests.* New York, 1931. Publisher is author. Report of the President and of the Treasurer for year ended September 30, 1931, pp. 45–62. Imprint is Carnegie Corporation.

————. "Resolution B–367: Ten Year Program in Library Service," Report of the President and Treasurer for the year ended September 30, 1926, pp. 47–48. Imprint is Carnegie Corporation.

Lester, Robert M. *Review of Grants for Library Interests, 1911–1935.* Printed for the Information of the Trustees of the Carnegie Corporation. New York, 1935. Office of the Secretary. Review Series 19.

Library School of the New York Public Library: Register, 1911–1926. New York: The New York Public Library, 1929.

Munn, Ralph. *Conditions and Trends in Education for Librarianship.* A report on the Program in Training for Library Service Adopted by the Board of Trustees of Carnegie Corporation of New York, March 19, 1926, together with the Report of Committee on Library Training, November, 1934—and other documents. Carnegie Corporation of New York, 5th Avenue, 1936. Imprint Carnegie Corporation. pp. 5–7 in the report of the meeting at Richmond.

Williamson, Charles C. *Annual Report of the Director of the School of Library Service.* Columbia University Information Bulletin, 1927.

———. *Training for Library Service.* A report prepared for the Carnegie Corporation of New York. Boston: Merrymount Pr., 1923.

UNPUBLISHED MATERIAL

Association of American Library Schools. "Minutes and Proceedings, 1923." Mimeographed. Urbana, Ill.: Univ. of Illinois, Graduate Library School.

———. "Minutes of the Meeting Held December 29, 1928." Mimeographed. Urbana, Ill.: Univ. of Illinois, Graduate Library School.

———. "Minutes of the Meeting Held May 13, 1929." Mimeographed. Urbana, Ill.: Univ. of Illinois, Graduate Library School.

———. "Proceedings." (December 30, 1929). Mimeographed. Urbana, Ill.: Univ. of Illinois, Graduate Library School.

———. "Proceedings." (December 29, 1930). Mimeographed. Urbana, Ill.: Univ. of Illinois, Graduate Library School.

———. "Proceedings." (June 24–25, 1931). Mimeographed. Urbana, Ill.: Univ. of Illinois, Graduate Library School.

———. "Proceedings." (December 1931). Mimeographed. Urbana, Ill.: Univ. of Illinois, Graduate Library School.

———. "Proceedings." (April 1932). Mimeographed. Urbana, Ill.: Univ. of Illinois, Graduate Library School.

———. "Report of Meetings." (June 13, 1938). Mimeographed. Urbana, Ill.: Univ. of Illinois, Graduate Library School.

Coulter, Edith M. "The Future of the Association of American Library Schools." Mimeographed. Report of meeting, May 10, 1936, of American Association of Library Schools at Richmond, Virginia.

Joeckel, C. B. "Supply and Demand in the Library Profession." Mimeographed. *Proceedings of the American Association of Library Schools*, Dec. 1931.

Munn, Ralph. "The Objectives of the Association of American Library Schools." Mimeographed. Report of meeting, May 10, 1936, of American Association of Library Schools at Richmond, Virginia.

Index